Praise for
BLESSING YOUR
CHILDREN

Our eternal Father desperately longs to bless
His children. And, as the creator of the parent-
child relationship, He knows how to give the
ultimate gifts. *Blessing Your Children* has articulated
many of God's unique favors. It teaches parents
to enjoy this intimate heavenly relationship and
pass those loves, opportunities, freedoms and
fulfillments on to their own children. The call
to bless our children is a divine assignment;
and with the grace of God and the help of the
Holy Spirit, we can pass on an inheritance
that will never fade.

GARY SMALLEY
MARRIAGE AND FAMILY AUTHOR,
THE GIFT OF THE BLESSING, LOVE IS A DECISION,
AND *KEY TO YOUR CHILD'S HEART*
WWW.SMALLEYONLINE.COM

Blessing Your Children is more than a book for
parents; it is for all of us who care about the next
generation. Pastor Jack has extended his hand
of blessing to touch me at many critical points
in my life. The impression he has left on me
will be visible for eternity. Let us take the
practical wisdom of *Blessing Your Children*
beyond our own homes to touch the lives of
every child within our reach.

LISA WELCHEL
ACTRESS AND AUTHOR, *CREATIVE CORRECTION* AND
THE FACTS OF LIFE AND OTHER LESSONS MY FATHER TAUGHT ME
CASTAIC, CALIFORNIA

BLESSING
Your
CHILDREN

JACK W. HAYFORD

Regal

From Gospel Light
Ventura, California, U.S.A.

Regal

PUBLISHED BY REGAL BOOKS
VENTURA, CALIFORNIA, U.S.A.
PRINTED IN THE U.S.A.

Regal Books is a ministry of Gospel Light, an evangelical Christian publisher dedicated to serving the local church. We believe God's vision for Gospel Light is to provide church leaders with biblical, user-friendly materials that will help them evangelize, disciple and minister to children, youth and families.

It is our prayer that this Regal book will help you discover biblical truth for your own life and help you meet the needs of others. May God richly bless you.

For a free catalog of resources from Regal Books/Gospel Light, please call your Christian supplier or contact us at 1-800-4-GOSPEL *or* www.regalbooks.com.

Rights for publishing this book in other languages are contracted by Gospel Light Worldwide, the international nonprofit ministry of Gospel Light. Gospel Light Worldwide also provides publishing and technical assistance to international publishers dedicated to producing Sunday School and Vacation Bible School curricula and books in the languages of the world. For additional information, visit www.gospellightworldwide.org; write to Gospel Light Worldwide, P.O. Box 3875, Ventura, CA 93006; or send an e-mail to info@gospellightworldwide.org.

Cover and interior design by Robert Williams
Edited by Kathi Mills and Deena Davis

Library of Congress Cataloging-in-Publication Data
Hayford, Jack W.
  Blessing your children / Jack W. Hayford.
    p.   cm.
  ISBN 0-8307-3079-6
    1. Parenting—Religious aspects—Christianity. 2. Child rearing—Religious aspects—Christianity. 3. Parenting—Biblical teaching. 4. Child rearing—Biblical teaching. 5. Blessing and cursing in the Bible. 6. Parents—Prayer-books and devotions—English. I. Title.
    BV4529 .H39 2002
    248.8'45—dc21   2002012979

1 2 3 4 5 6 7 8 9 10 / 09 08 07 06 05 04 03 02

CONTENTS

FOREWORD

I am one of Pastor Jack Hayford's spiritual kids—his daughter in the Lord. That's because 32 years ago, at a very low point in my life, Pastor Jack talked to me about Jesus and the life that God had for me. I ended up receiving the Lord in his office. For the next 23 years, I attended Church On The Way where Jack was the pastor, and I grew up in the things of the Lord under his teaching. The foundations of my life were solidly established during the time I spent there.

One of those foundations was becoming the kind of parent that God wanted me to be. Because of my own dysfunctional upbringing—I was raised by a mentally ill mother who was abusive and by a father who could not control my mother's cruelty—I didn't have good role models for parenting when my own children were born. I knew I was not equipped to raise them. But I was able to learn everything I needed to know about that from Pastor Jack.

I learned, first of all, by example as I watched Pastor Jack and Anna raise their four wonderful children. I never saw trouble or rebellion in any of the children as they grew up to be solid and grounded in the things of God. I was even more impressed when I saw the high-quality person each one of them chose to marry. And I continue to be impressed with the great children *they* in turn are raising. It was clear that this was a family who knew what worked.

I also learned how to be a godly parent from Pastor Jack's teachings on the subject. One of the most important things he taught was how to bless and speak life into a child. I came to understand that we all have the power to plant seeds, not only in the hearts of our own children, but also in any child God brings into our lives. These seeds can produce good fruit or they can produce weeds that choke out life. The things we say can live in a child's heart for a lifetime and mold the way they think about themselves and the people around them. We can either point children toward a path of self-destruction or help them to find the destiny God has for them.

That is what this book is all about. In a culture that has lost all sense of what is best for a child, Pastor Jack boldly speaks the truth. In a society that too often devalues children or overindulges them, or uses them for self-gratification, he shows us how we can have a powerful effect for good. He shows us how to speak words that bring life and not death, blessings and not curses, encouragement and not discouragement. He shows us how to build up and not tear down. This book will help you leave a spiritual inheritance to your children that will serve them well for a lifetime.

Stormie Omartian
Author, *The Power of a Praying Parent*

Chapter One

From GENERATION *to* GENERATION

One generation shall praise Your works to another,
and shall declare Your mighty acts.

PSALM 145:4

It was several years ago, while I flew across the Atlantic
toward Africa where I was scheduled to speak to a group
of church leaders, that I began to read a book concerning
planning for the future. One of the foremost decisions
borne of that reading was that it motivated my wife, Anna,

and me to do the one thing it said we should do immediately if we hadn't already done so—prepare a will. With the help of one of the attorneys in our church, we began to work through the details of our children's inheritance.

An Inheritance for Your Children

A good man leaves an inheritance to his children's children.
Proverbs 13:22

The matter of inheritance—both spiritual and material—is addressed throughout the Old and New Testaments. Depending upon a man's godly wisdom (or his foolishness), his descendants might inherit anything from prosperity to folly. Our spiritual inheritance, "willed" to us as adopted sons and daughters of God through Jesus Christ, is described in Matthew 25:34 as "the kingdom [of God] prepared for [us] from the foundation of the world." While the book you are now holding in your hands and the one I read on the plane are very different, they are similar in more ways than one might think, because they parallel the matter of establishing a will and transmitting an inheritance.

The will Anna and I prepared to make, with the help of our attorney, was a conscious judgment that would state how the inheritance of what we have will someday be distributed to those we love. Since the combined value of all a person's assets is referred to as his or her net worth, I remember thinking it especially gracious of the attorney that, as he totaled what Anna and I owned, he didn't refer to it as our "net worthlessness." As a couple, at that time in our late forties, we were not in debt; but the amalgamate sum of our earthly possessions reflected the fact that we had pursued the path of pastoral ministry—one seldom known for an accumulation of wealth.

As we looked over the paperwork together, the attorney—highly respected in his profession and also a man of deep commitment to Jesus Christ—made such a gentle, touching observation. Rather than make a condescending remark about our small estate, he simply said, "Well, Pastor Hayford, just studying these figures, it's clear to see where you have set your priorities." It might have been a nice way of exclaiming, "Wow, this is pathetic. A guy your age ought to have a lot more money than this." But I don't believe that's what he meant. He knew enough of Anna's and my life to know how gracious the Lord has been to us. He knew of the multitudinous ways we've been blessed—in our marriage, in our family, in our ministry and in the privilege of seeing so many lives touched, changed and enriched over the years. And while being in ministry for our whole life together has certainly not made us financially wealthy,

Anna and I have no complaints. At that moment, and even to this hour, if we could start all over again, we would do it exactly the same way.

After the will had finally been drawn up, Anna and I were able to arrange a setting in which we could review the will with our kids. Of course, we had few assets and no idea of what a future date would afford them as their inheritance, but we nonetheless went over the details, explaining the formula by which anything we had would one day be passed on to them.

Learning and planning how to transmit blessing to our children involves as real a decision as arranging their inheritance of material things via a will.

That day in our living room offers a genuine and practical spiritual parallel to this book's subject of blessing your children, for learning and planning how to transmit blessing to them involves as real a decision as arranging their inheritance of material things via a will.

I thought of that as I began writing. Just as that attorney was a spokesperson for what human law requires, I wondered if Father God would let me be a spokesman for His laws—His "ways that work for human benefit" (see Rom. 8:28). That's what God's laws are about—all of them.

And I'm hoping to help parents and others think about and plan how they can pass life's greatest inheritance to the children in their lives. More precious than any material sum, the values of love, understanding, enriched relationship and spiritual blessing *can* and *should be* transmitted. In much the same way as that family meeting in our living room, our heavenly Father God is ready to show us His will designed not only to bless us with the inheritance of His goodness in our lives but also to pass on as blessings to our kids.

And incidentally, it's worth noting that there's a distinctive beauty in the difference between God's will and the will Anna and I reviewed with our children. A human will can wind up being mishandled by a shyster attorney. When someone dies and thus is obviously not there to govern the administration of or give explanation concerning the will, confusion and misdistribution can occur. But when we seek to live in God's will and relay it to our children, we enter another arena—one of great certainty that what we are seeking to pass on can succeed in being realized for and in the next generation. Why? First, because Jesus died to make God's will possible for each of us—you, me, our children. We don't need to die to transmit the inheritance; He has already done it. And Jesus not only died on the cross to release the possibilities of God's will to us (and through us, as we influence our kids), but He also rose again and now has become the attorney executing God's will for our lives. Jesus is our "Advocate with the Father" (1 John 2:1)—the ultimate probate attorney—and having risen from the dead, He is at the Father's right hand, ministering for us and to us in order to assure our success when we seek to experience the Father's will, relay it to our children and let it shape their lives.

The Heritage of Solomon

Few places in the Bible are as rich as the book of Proverbs in illustrating the parameters of blessing our children. Solomon described his expectation of passing along to his own son the inheritance of wisdom and godly counsel he had received from his father, David:

> When I was my father's son, tender and the only one in the sight of my mother, He also taught me, and said to me: "Let your heart retain my words; keep my commands, and live" (Prov. 4:3-4).

This legacy was intended to be passed from generation to generation—including yours and mine. It is a legacy that contains the values, principles and formulas for successful, happy living and also the warnings regarding those things that bring misery and failure. In Proverbs, Solomon was seeking to relay instruction in God's wisdom and, with the teaching, explain the reason why it works. Connected to this wisdom is the warning of dire consequences if the foundations are not firmly laid in child rearing by establishing and applying the principle of godly discipline and correction of children. Solomon advises his son:

> My son, do not despise the chastening of the LORD, nor detest His correction; for whom the LORD loves He corrects, just as a father the son in whom he delights (3:11-12).

As parents, we can gain a measure of comfort in noting that neither David nor Solomon was perfect. In fact, both men experienced severe failure by reason of violating their own counsel. Nonetheless, through their repentance they were restored and, beyond their human failure, the Psalms (most written by David's hand) and Proverbs (most written by Solomon's hand) remain today as evidence of their commitment and devotion to God and His ways.

David and Solomon's fallibility as human beings did not prevent them from handing down a spiritual and moral legacy to their children. The message? Whenever you or I may be tempted to doubt our capacity to bring a lasting, worthy influence on the children whose lives we touch, or feel intimidated by our own sense of inadequacy or by our past, we have these vivid examples from Scripture to encourage us. Through God's grace and forgiveness and by our willingness to confront our shortcomings and failures as parents, as well as by our earnest desire and devotion to bless our children by relating to them on God's terms and with His wisdom, we can succeed in blessing our children.

There is no reason for any adult believer reading this book to think that you are disqualified from the possibility of becoming a true "blesser" of your kids. Let me share with you from my own experience.

The Example of My Parents

September is a milestone in the history of my family, for on the twenty-eighth day of that month, over a half century ago, a young couple discovered the love of God in Jesus Christ: Jack and Dolores Hayford, my parents, gave their lives to Him. Two weeks later, according to the Word of God, they presented me, their one-year-old firstborn, in dedication to the Lord at a worship service in Long Beach, California. They were already beginning to discover how to establish their lives and their home in God's order. In accordance with the timeless biblical tradition—from the Old Testament into the New—they brought their child for presentation to the Lord.

In the years to follow, I was reared in the ways of the Lord, but it is important to point out something that may seem curiously contradictory. Simply put, our home was not a "religious" home. Oh, to be sure, it was a very vital and loving family environment. Spiritual values governed our lives. But while the principles of Christian discipleship were common to our household, the rigidity, legalism or austere mood often imagined or depicted when a religious home is described were very absent. In fact, notwithstanding the positive qualities I remember, let me add to what may already seem quite peculiar. There were actually a few years when my father, struggling with his own walk with God, refused to go to church. Yet even then, my dad always respected the ways of the Lord, making sure that prayer was reverent and meaningful at table times and that we kids regularly attended Sunday School. We learned to tithe—just as Daddy and Mamma did, even in the years when Dad was backslidden.

> *I was reared in the ways of the Lord, but our home was not a "religious" home.*

The blessing of being raised in a home that is established according to God's ways is an immeasurable gift—one that I received along with my younger sister and brother. My parents read the Bible and taught us to do the same. They would teach us what they were learning of God's grace and truth with a practical approach that made His ways seem desirable—something we would want to do. This was so much the case that, at the time, we didn't even realize we were being taught godly principles. Instead, spirituality was simply made a natural part of a warm reality—the practical, livable lifestyle that made up the fabric of our home. Because of our lifestyle, people often called us church people; but church was never a substitute for what was taking place in our home. Church never is.

The Stewardship of Potential

The earliest blessing a child can receive from those influencing his or her life is to answer the question, How can I cultivate an atmosphere of God's order and love in our home and form an understanding mind-set that life is not to be lived for oneself but in the interest of others?

This mind-set, of course, requires that those who will potentially bless the child be open to the Holy Spirit's application of God's Word and Jesus' ways in their lives, as well as to becoming people who, being shaped by the

Savior, are equipped to pass God's life on to the next generation. Admittedly, this way of living doesn't suit the tastes of the flesh. It runs contrary to the world's me-centered lifestyle; but it is the Lord's way, and it works. Put into practice, it will continue to work effectively from generation to generation.

This concept is as old as God's covenant with Abraham—a promise He made to bless Abraham personally; better still, God promised that through this blessing Abraham would bless innumerable others in generations to come. "In your seed all the nations of the earth shall be blessed, because you have obeyed My voice" (Gen. 22:18). It is in the light of this truth and Abraham's model that we now approach the potential that you and I seek to realize in our lives.

The theme before us addresses blessing your children, but it's not only a book for parents and grandparents or even solely for people who have a child in their immediate home. The blessing of children is within the grasp of almost every adult, a fact that holds the possibility of transforming the future of millions of kids who will otherwise experience the deficiencies or the trauma of an "unblessed" life.

Virtually every one of us has been given, in one way or another, *the stewardship of a potential*—the possibility of providing good, positive, spiritual, healthy and worthy blessings upon the children whom the Lord has placed in our lives. Our own healthy view of this opportunity will also help us to see how it is every believer's responsibility to bless our children. Our failure to bless the children in our lives holds significant and serious consequences for them now, in their ongoing future and, ultimately, for our whole world. To shape a child for tomorrow is to shape tomorrow's world, and to shape a child in God's wholesome order of blessing is to multiply the same to that child's entire realm of future influence. It is the same thing as bequeathing an inheritance to the next generation.

To shape a child for tomorrow is to shape tomorrow's world.

God's Heart as a Parent

While the Bible makes clear that "God is not a man, that He should lie" (Num. 23:19), it doesn't ever present God as distant from emotions that we feel ourselves. There are limits to paralleling God's feelings with ours, for there is a vast distance between the essence of His being and the nature of our own. Still, it is not unbiblical to see God's parental heart of passionate concern for His beloved creature, man.

For I, the LORD your God, am a jealous God, visiting the iniquity of the fathers upon the children to the third and fourth generations of those who hate Me, but showing mercy to thousands, to those who love Me and keep My commandments (Exod. 20:5-6).

To parent with faith, we need to regain touch with the practical reality that God fully understands our frustrations and occasional sorrow as parents.

Make no mistake: those are not vindictive words but words of commitment. God declares His passion, His jealousy—the emotion that exhibits a refusal to allow the violation of what properly belongs to a person. He indicates that His penalties for sin are not merely punitive but are also intended to alert and awaken those who wander: He wants them back. His pensive care is shown to their obedience, not because His children have earned it, but because His love is so inescapably bound to them.

To parent with faith we need to learn the heart of the ultimate parent; we need to regain touch with the practical reality that God fully understands our frustrations and occasional sorrow as parents.

Judith came to my office one day, seeking counsel for dealing with a very trying season she was experiencing with her 20-year-old daughter, Alicia, whom she had raised by herself after her husband, Alicia's father, had left the family. As is often the case, Judith's lack of wise parenting in Alicia's early years had resulted in an adult daughter who was tangled in bondage—her behavior was manipulative, self-willed and rebellious. Judith's own upbringing had been by loving but uninformed parents who transferred the brokenness and inadequacies of their childhood to her. Further, Judith had not come to know the Lord until Alicia was a teenager. Though Judith's new birth and growth in Christ was genuine, she found it a very difficult process to apply what Jesus had done in her life and at the same time bring full-measured remedy to the deficiencies in the upbringing of her daughter's already-formed personality.

One day after a particularly brutal verbal battle in which Alicia had pushed every emotional button she could to hurt her mother's feelings, Judith told me she went to her knees to cry out to the Lord.

"Oh, Father God," she began, "I know You don't have to deal with these kinds of horrible things . . ." Her intent had obviously been to declare her trust in God, regardless of what she faced; but her words exhibited an erroneous perception that her problems had no parallel in heaven. She later told me the somewhat humorous outcome of her prayerful encounter.

Judith described the feeling of suddenly being stopped in midsentence, as if God were holding the words she had just spoken in front of her while gently laughing and impressing her heart with these words: "Oh, I don't, do I? You say I don't know what it means to have to deal with rebellious, ungrateful, spite-filled children?" The instant the impression came, Judith was overcome with laughter. She almost wept with laughter's tears—and because of the Father's gracious prompting—and patience—with her misperception. She was clearly informed: Of course God understands our sense of being limited by things our kids do; He faces the same thing daily!

Never forget that Father God—King of the universe, creator of all things, and reigning on the throne of heaven—is also a parent. Can He identify with the parental anguish we feel at times?

- Have you ever provided an opportunity, sought to do something special, prepared a dinner, furnished a room or bought something for a child who then misused or ruined it? Consider God's feelings after having made all things in excellence and perfection in Eden's garden and then watching His created child Adam trash it all through disobedience.

- Have you ever been called to sacrifice something you held precious in order to help your kids solve a problem or exit a situation blocking their future? Consider creation's physical evidence of the Father's feelings when incredible darkness covered the earth during the Crucifixion. Feel the creator's grieving agony, see the shadow darkening the world as a reminder that His parent heart suffered as His Son, Jesus, was crucified on the cross to pay the debt for our sins.

Like us, God both delights in His children and suffers over them. His heart breaks at their disobedience—but not because He wants to control them. On the contrary, the whole reason Adam was able to sin in the first place was because of the enormous liability inherent in God's unconditional love that gave Adam the free will to choose. Our heavenly parent feels sorrow for His children's mistakes and rebellion, just as you and I do, because He knows what pathway can best bring us to genuine fulfillment and happiness in our lives, and He sees the dead end before we've even set foot on the road.

Just as our Father God goes through these things with His sons and daughters, He calls us to become vessels of His parental love and guidance to the children in our lives. In order to do that, we have to know what is in His will, His heart and His Word—and we need to start applying this knowledge early. While results are not beyond reach in later years, the most effective approach is to learn and obey God's ways of teaching and training our children and thereby blessing them by taking action while they are young.

Children and the Things of God

Many people are unaware that the idea of guardian angels is taught in the Bible. It is not based in superstition nor born of mythology; and it is far more than poetry. Psalm 91:11 declares, "He shall give His angels charge over you." Hebrews 1:14 describes angels as "ministering spirits sent forth to minister for those who will inherit salvation." Look at their protective action in Bible case studies:

- An angel stepped in to save and preserve the life of Jesus as Joseph and Mary were instructed to leave Bethlehem with the child (see Matt. 2:13).
- An angel entered the cell where Peter was imprisoned and led him to freedom (see Acts 12:7-11).

- An angel came to Paul as he was caught up in a hurricane on the Mediterranean Sea (see Acts 27:23-24).

Angels are active throughout the Scriptures, and they continue in their activity with the people of God to this day. It is with good reason that we sing Bill and Gloria Gaither's lyrics about hearing the brush of angels' wings as a sort of announcement and reminder of the Lord's presence. Angels are a spiritual reality, and what Jesus said about them as it relates to our children (see Matt. 18:1-14) is important to understand.

Take heed that you do not despise one of these little ones, for I say to you that in heaven their angels always see the face of My Father who is in heaven (v. 10).

In this particular passage, where Jesus was instructing a group of disciples in the importance of valuing and protecting the simplicity, beauty and innocence of a child, He made an important observation. In speaking of those guardian angels assigned to the care of each child, His words about the posture of these angels toward God tells us something. The fact that they "always see the face of My Father" suggests that the disposition of children in their innocence is naturally open toward the things of God. It is as though the Lord was saying these angels had not yet been embarrassed by the attitudes or actions of their earthling charges; nor were they yet having to battle demonic enterprises voluntarily submitted to by these charges. Jesus' words underscore the spiritual vulnerability of children and, with it, their ready availability and openness to the Lord.

Studies have shown that a vast majority of Christians receive Jesus Christ before they enter teenage years. I remember when my brother, Jim, received Jesus. He's 10 years younger than I am and is a gifted pastor ministering in the Seattle area. But when he was five years old, he watched a children's presentation on a Christian telecast. A heart with a little door on it appeared on the TV screen. The teacher quoted Revelation 3:20 and then said, "If you will open the door and let Jesus come in, He will." And Jim did. If you ask my brother today—a mature spiritual leader of a congregation numbering well over 4,000—he will tell you, "I received Jesus Christ and was born again when I was five years old."

My mother made a decision for Christ with full adult awareness when she was 19, but her testimony was this: "When I was four years old, a woman told me about Jesus when our family lived in Colorado. I remember that I didn't completely understand, but I knew I wanted what she was talking about and opened myself as well as I knew how, with no Christian-home background." She was sure that the "bending of the twig" at that early age paved the way to her later decision when she and my father heard the gospel shortly after their marriage.

Let it be fixed in our hearts: The innocence, openness and vulnerability of children make them receptive to knowing Jesus at a young age. These qualities also make them uniquely shapable to the Lord's ways if parents and other adults can be found who will commit to blessing them. Children who are blessed by the adults in their lives have the opportunity for a full lifetime to know and grow in the joy, wisdom and benefits of learning the Lord's ways. They are certain to become a returned blessing to their parents and have a destiny, by God's grace, to deliver that blessing to others around them.

The Beginning of Wisdom

My son . . . keep sound wisdom and discretion; so they will be life to your soul and grace to your neck.
PROVERBS 3:21-22

The Bible offers us much practical guidance regarding the value of instruction; but the incarnation of wisdom in a child's soul—the kind that "take[s] root downward and bear[s] fruit upward" (2 Kings 19:30; Isa. 37:31)—only happens by the power of the Holy Spirit.

The children you and I can influence are more open to the things of the Spirit than adults often realize. When we help to form in them a passion for God's Word and the fullness of His Spirit early on, we can equip them to choose between right and wrong, between good and evil, between a living future or a dead-end street—as those choices will most certainly present themselves. To accomplish this formation requires two things of us: (1) to answer the call and act with confidence, believing that blessing our children is a divine assignment, and (2) to let God fulfill the assignment by His divine grace and ability.

The basic reality is this: To be a blessing to our children, we simply need to become childlike ourselves—to believe God's call and to receive God's grace for the task. So let us now set forward together.

What you will now read is intended to offer practical, godly ways of blessing our children by transmitting a heavenly, incorruptible and undefiled inheritance (see 1 Pet. 1:4) to our biological children, our adoptive children or any children the Lord has entrusted to us so that we might make them spiritual heirs of God's best for their lives.

From the wellspring of my own years as both a child and a parent and from the base of nearly five decades of pastoral ministry to my spiritual heirs—the congregation I've served and the pastors I've nurtured—I offer this book. It contains the basics of what I have found of God's practical ways for blessing the children in your life. It will run the gamut, from dealing with the need to teach children to respect and listen to their parents to showing them how to cultivate their own dynamic, personal relationship with Father God through the living Savior, Jesus Christ. Since God has assigned us this heritage-transmitting task that has such temporal and eternal consequences that will determine whether our children will be prepared to deliver the same to their next generation, let's study together.

Father God—the ultimate parent—will grant the mercies of His kindness and the power of His Spirit to enable us because He loves those children so deeply Himself. That's why He has assigned us to help them—to guide and to shape them toward spiritual, moral and social victory . . . or failure. Let's prepare with sensitivity and with hope so that faithful, fruitful, fulfilled and productive children will become the "fruit" by which we, as parents, are known (see Matt. 7:20).

Prayer

Father God, I realize today that the greatest blessing I can pass along to the children in my life is the one You've given me—Your life-giving Word and Your life-living Holy Spirit, which I inherited by the activation of Your will at Calvary. Thank You, Lord, that I needn't die to share this inheritance because it was paid for by Your own Son, Jesus Christ. Your gift of Kingdom life to me is a blessing that only grows the more I give it to others. Like the blessing You gave to Abraham, I pray that the spiritual inheritance I impart to the children in my life would multiply greatly from generation to generation and that over their lifetimes, my children would be the bearers of much godly fruit. In Jesus' name, I pray. Amen.

Chapter Two

BLESS YOUR
CHILDREN WITH A
LONG AND
FRUITFUL LIFE

*Honor your father and your mother, that your days may be long
upon the land which the LORD your God is giving you.*

EXODUS 20:12

There can hardly be any parents alive who do not expect
their children to outlive them, nor any parents who do not

wish a successful life for those children. So it shouldn't surprise us that God feels exactly the same way. In fact, within the content of the Ten Commandments He has carved His desire and readiness to bless our children with exactly that—a long and successful life.

As we read Exodus 20:12, as it appears above, it becomes beautifully clear that God has offered a way that a child may be open to a full life both in years ("that your days may be long") and in adequacy ("upon the land"). The latter phrase refers to the promised arena of God blessing you, and your fruitfulness. This is why Ephesians 6:1-3 not only brings the counsel of this commandment's wisdom into a New Testament exhortation but also refers to these words as "the first commandment with promise" (v. 3). The essential truth is this: If children honor their fathers and mothers, they are functioning within God's order in such a way that the inheritance of a full and fruitful life—the very dimensions of life that God wants each person to know (see Jer. 29:11)—will be unhindered.

Hereby we are introduced to a foundational life principle, one that God has woven into the fabric of the universe: You cannot dishonor your parents and still realize fruitfulness or fullness in life to the dimension that God intended for you. Life—for everyone involved—is inevitably diminished if children are not taught to honor their parents. Everyone loses something if a child is not led by love and taught the practical ways that characterize God's intended wisdom and care, which beget a recognition of God's expectation to manifest respect for and display obedience toward parental relationship and authority. How can we do this and thereby bless our children?

Blessing Through Instruction and Correction

As with so many issues of discipleship facing believers in God's Word and His Son, Jesus, the opportunities for knowing the benevolent blessings in God's covenant ways will often bring us into confrontation with the world's mind-set.

There has been a trend in popular society over the last several decades for parents to become more like friends to their children than to accept the role of parent, which essentially calls us to an accountable exercise of instruction and authority. Simply being pals or supposing we can relate to our kids as equals may sound very friendly and democratic. But even though God never negates the joys of closeness with our children or the worthiness of cultivating their self-respect by showing them that graciousness, let no parent be misguided. The parental call is to train the child, shape the child and correct and instruct the child. To fail to do these things, however chummy we may think we are with our children, results in the frightening possibility that such worldly minded tactics will leave a child standing alone, without the necessary social, domestic and spiritual mentoring.

It's one thing to open the door to good times for children by taking them fishing, but only a fool will leave them in the boat by themselves. Similarly, being pals and having fun with our kids may have its place, but the bottom line is that parents are the ones whom God has made responsible to train up a child in the way that he or she should go (see Prov. 22:6). Put another way, "fun parents" may play catch with their children or even arrange for them to register for Little League participation, but a coach will still be needed to show them how to play.

> *It's one thing to open the door to good times for children by taking them fishing, but only a fool will leave them in the boat by themselves.*

Parents are the ones who need to oversee the shaping of proper attitudes toward competition, teammates, the distinction between accepting the benefits and disciplines of a sport and not becoming caught up in the need to win or supposing a bad temper is justified if something doesn't go their way. It is this very role—as the mentor who teaches honor for relational values—that will form children who learn and accept God's commandment to honor their parents.

The Word of God clearly states that "a child left to himself brings shame to his mother" (Prov. 29:15). In short, children who are not raised to honor parents will tend to regard their intended inheritance—of parental wisdom, instruction, correction and spiritual insight—as irrelevant. Such an atmosphere breeds the strong likelihood that children will become disrespectful, impolite, smart-faced, wisecracking, tantrum-prone screamers when upset and will talk back with expected impunity, vainly bound by the idea that the world exists for their convenience. Too many kids, lacking a parent's proper care and influence, are creating chaos in homes today, where God's order has not been established because children have been left to themselves.

Where parents willingly or ignorantly allow such patterns of dishonor, they are daily contributing to an eventual deprivation of their children. A child's failure to learn honor can manifest over time and in many ways—even socially accepted ways. But God's promised blessings of long life and success are directly related to parents' acceptance of the task of cultivating in their children a right heart attitude toward them.

The alternative to the promise is enough to motivate us: Failure to foster our children's learning in the areas of parental honor, authority and respect invites the inverse of the promise—life cut short, both in years and in quality. The seriousness of the issue calls us to see God's commandment as filled with either wonderful or destructive potential. We are either shaping a child toward hope under development or we are forsaking them to a heartbreak in the making.

Cultivating Honor

The essence of the idea of the word "honor" has to do with the weightiness of worth ascribed to the object being honored. It is the basic idea behind our call to worship God. Of course, this is not to propose the ridiculous idea that we teach our children to worship us as parents. But an understanding of their place must be shaped in children, not to reduce their possible attainment, but to release it. Just as nothing makes life work better than finding our place in proper relationship to God, so teaching children to revere their parents—to give appropriate weight to who we are in their lives—will bring long-term benefits. This doesn't come by passivity, and it certainly doesn't come by permissiveness. Honor is a concept that adults can and must help children to exhibit—toward parents, toward elders, toward authority figures, toward other ethnicities, toward leaders and toward friends. It starts with how parents are treated—and you and I are the ones who set the pace for determining what that treatment will mean.

The chain had long since broken, but what remained had become part of the tree and would never come out.

I know a host of parental couples and singles, grandparents and surrogate parents, who have cultivated their children to show honor to them and to others. The results: The kids are more (not less) confident about themselves; they have been raised to learn their place. And with that, the kids also hold their parents in tremendous honor, not because it was ground into them by threats, but because it was *grown* into them by a balanced mix of love and authority.

Anna and I recently visited a member of our church who has a huge pecan tree in her backyard. It was spectacular—more than two stories high and home to dozens of squirrels and birds. Early on in the tree's development—it had been planted more than 50 years ago—it had forked into two main trunks, and a heavy chain had been hooked around them, so they wouldn't split as the tree grew. In time, the girth of the tree's trunks had thickened and grown around the chain so that now it was imbedded. The chain had long since broken, but what remained had become part of the tree and would never come out.

Cultivating honor in a child is much like that. What we plant in our children grows with them until it becomes a part of them. That will be the case with ungodly values as well as with godly—so we must not leave children to themselves. Like the chain in the tree, children who learn to honor their parents will find that wisdom holds something together within them. And, equally, if children are allowed to form a loathing or disrespect for their parents, it will end in a loathing and hatred for themselves.

There is a huge responsibility upon us in all this, an issue clearly emphasized in Ephesians 6:4:

> And you, fathers, do not provoke your children to wrath, but bring them up in the training and admonition of the Lord.

The Bible gives us clearly assigned parameters. Parents who desire to teach their children to honor them must also see that parental authority is not a privileged "bossdom."

Instead, we are called to lead, live, teach, train and relate to our children in a manner that engenders that honor. We must beget it in them. It cannot be taught by demand alone, but still there is an assigned component in a child's training process that requires parents to draw the boundaries of respect.

Our children may respond defiantly to things that we say, but that doesn't mean we have the right to speak to them in a crude, coarse or unloving manner. We are instructed by the Word of God not to provoke them in any way that would be inconsiderate, mean or ungracious. Further, as shapers of their attitudes, we are explicitly told not to inflict bad attitudes on children. Our kids may get irritated when, within the proper limits of the training process, they are told to do things they don't want to do. But that's different than provoking them to wrath.

Understanding the Why Behind the Rules

The word "admonition" relates to reasonableness, being derived from the Greek word for "mind." The idea is that we should train our children so that they understand the issues behind what we tell them to do. This is not a matter of apologizing by saying "I'm sorry, but I just have to require this." It is a matter of teaching (admonishing) by saying "There are good reasons for this, and I want you to get the picture." In that regard, please be patient with this bold assertion: I believe there is one reason you should never give to your child for the rules you apply, the principles you teach or the corrective action you take. Never explain it all by saying "Our church doesn't believe in that and that's why we do or don't do (whatever it is you are instructing or correcting about)." To base any requirements on grounds other than your own God-given authority and your convictions about His Word is to suggest your own uncertainty about the validity of whatever point you are making. If cheap reasons are given, however high-sounding, don't be surprised if your kids rebel or end up away from God and godliness.

The call of the text is to train our kids by giving them boldly yet graciously communicated and intelligent, sensible, well-described reasons for the things expected and required of them. Teach them the ideas behind what they can and cannot do, framing your words with good-sense explanations. Be mindful to explain that your reasons for "doing it right" are wise (1) in the light of our long-range best interests as human beings and (2) in the light of the Word of God that you are heeding as you "bring them up in the training and admonition of the Lord."

When there is a quest to honor God, He is faithful to compensate for whatever our imperfections in making the attempt. His redemptive grace will step into even those situations where we as parents fail and we provoke our children, whether by anger born of frustration or by our firmness in the face of a situation that might have been compromised. The Lord's commandment to parents is to teach our children to honor the human vehicle (parents) by which He brought them into the world, and to be forgiving toward them. So when both children and parents honestly seek to live with a full accountability to God's Word, be assured that He not only assists us in our pursuit but, as a result, He will honor us with His gracious, promised release of all fullness and fruitfulness in our lives.

Training That Leads to Blessing

In my book *Living the Spirit-Formed Life*, I wrote about the disciplines of Christian living that define a disciple of the Lord Jesus Christ. Children need spiritual disciplines too. Children who grow up accustomed to family life that includes prayer, worship, reading the Bible and listening for the Lord's voice when they find themselves faced with a dilemma will grow into healthy, mature men and women of God who are able to make good decisions and are equipped to be a blessing to others. Such disciplines of true discipleship are not religious strictures or legalistic rules that choke the life out of a believer—child or adult. Rather, they are the basis for practical spiritual growth, proven through the years and workable at some dimension in the life of any believer, irrespective of age.

I first began to learn the same disciplines I write and teach about today when I was a boy. These disciplines are formative dynamics that help us grow into agents of God's love and redemptive will. So I encourage you to pursue them, setting the model for your children. Then use those dynamics to teach your kids. For example, teach them how to confess sin and be rid of it, what repentance really means and how to practice it, how to forgive others and why that discipline is so key to truly liberated living. Encourage your children to recognize the need for these and other disciplines as their natural growth and understanding might recommend. Watch for circumstances—teaching moments—when an easy entrance into such themes may afford blessing your children with lessons in living as a disciple of Jesus. The result will be a reward in itself—Anna and I rejoice in it constantly, not only in watching the truth of one of God's promises illustrated in our four children today, but also in seeing them succeed in doing the same with our grandchildren. That fulfilled promise is found in Proverbs 22:6:

> Train up a child in the way he should go, and when he is old he will not depart from it.

As the children of godly parents who taught us the place of Christian disciplines in our daily lives, Anna and I became parents to children who are now teaching those disciplines to their kids. It's a case of the blessing becoming an inheritance, as the Word of God declares.

Influencing Children for Better or Worse

We live in a society confused about what brings fulfillment of a person's potential. The world's mind-set argues that fulfillment is found in self-realization. In the world's view, man was created and evolved by chance. From this philosophical base emerges the belief that development into adulthood will also take place largely by chance. Consequently, the mood of the world can influence our thinking and encourage us to become passive, neglecting our responsibility to train our children by purposefully spending time, watching closely, teaching at timely moments and building into them the godly values and beliefs that will grow them into whole people

Though even the average worldling is faithful to respond to the parental instinct to provide for and protect our children physically and materially, too often what is overlooked is the spiritual dimension of their growth. In this regard, instead of guiding them into maturity, society has virtually deified the idea of a hands-off attitude, advising that we leave them to their own journey of self-discovery. This is considered broad-minded and described as generously allowing self-expression.

From a biblical perspective it is the narrowest of views, for it completely amputates the God-intended relationship of parent to child with reference to spiritual, moral and personal understanding. Don't be duped by the idea that "training up a child" is the production of a religious robot. No! When training is done with God's loving truth and ministered nonlegalistically—with a sensitivity to the Holy Spirit's way, work and timing—it will grow a child who indeed comes to true self-understanding and whose self-expression reflects the character of Christ begotten in them by their own choice and because they have learned from their parents the values and joys of such a lifestyle.

Accepting the Privilege
of Influence

All of us, whether parents or not, can and do influence the children within our sphere of contact. Each one of us was shaped by adult influences in our lives from infancy throughout childhood and into our teenage years. Whether our experience was one of joy or abuse, we were affected by it. Ultimately, we tend to project the influences of the adults we knew in our formative years, resulting either in an optimistic attitude toward life, an underlying bitterness or a determination not to behave in the same way. Just as some of the influences that shaped us were imperfect, so our expression of them is also tarnished as we relay them to another generation. This, too, becomes a form of inheritance; but it is more akin to inheriting our parents' debts than their assets.

Too often we adults fail to realize the influence we have upon children. That is amazing, especially in light of the fact that each of us remembers vividly how the words and actions of certain adults influenced us. Sometimes it was just a remark, seemingly insignificant to the adult, and yet it cut through us as sharply as a razor. On the other hand, it may have been a word of encouragement at an appropriate moment. In either case, just one word—

whether ill spoken or perfectly timed—can leave an imprint on a child's soul, an imprint that colors a lifetime of future behavior for better or for worse. Since we can each recall a moment from childhood when we were either inspired by an authority figure or violated by one—a parent, an older brother or sister, a teacher, a pastor—let us be sensitized to the fact that our influence is no less powerful. As adults we need to allow ourselves to be sensitized to our personal influence on the children in our lives and give place to the Holy Spirit to keep us available and aware to serve that influence in His way and by His gracious power.

One example of how I've watched adults exert a tender but dynamic touch on the lives of children is at The Church On The Way, where we train even the nursery workers to recognize the power of their personal touch on the babies in their care. Those who are part of that ministry are trained to believe in and exercise spiritual vitality and love in a way that can impart life to their young charges. By prayer, singing and speaking tender words—even sitting and rocking an infant—an infusion of the life of the Holy Spirit can flow from these workers into that baby. At the next age level the same is practiced: Even the smallest toddler who doesn't yet have the ability to listen to or understand a Sunday School lesson can be prayed over and blessed by an adult. Yes, my adult friend, whether you are a parent or not, the Holy Spirit can and is willing to use you to plant something into the lives of the children around you!

Changing Our Attitude Toward Children

The next time you encounter a child—whether that child is sitting in the seat of a grocery cart in front of yours at the supermarket checkout line or next to you at the family dinner table—consider that the way in which you relate and speak to that child could make a significant difference in his or her self-perception in years to come. Let me tell you of a change I learned that I needed to make in this regard.

Many years ago, when the Lord brought this particular issue to light, I, of course, had not been unkind to the many little ones I often encountered—nearly always when they were with their parents. But the Lord alerted me to the way I responded to children when they were with adults, initiating an experience that effected a considerable transformation in my behavior toward little children. It surprised me when He did this, because it caused me to realize that for many years during the first part of my ministry, whenever I saw somebody with a child, I would always greet the parent or adult but not child, unless it was an older child of perhaps high school age. I would hardly notice or acknowledge the child—especially a very young, small child. Even worse was that it never crossed my mind that the child might, consciously or unconsciously, sense my inattentiveness and, thereby, I might contribute to a gradual inclination of the child to minimize his or her own worth.

I had not been unkind to the many little ones I often encountered— but the Lord alerted me to the way I responded to children when they were with adults.

When my failure was brought to my attention by the Holy Spirit, I felt badly enough to imagine that even one child might have felt unimportant to me. I felt even worse when I thought about how many children (and adults) relate to a pastor the way they do to God. I was shaken to the core by this self-discovery of a neglectful habit: Children (or adults) could interpret my passivity toward them as being the way God felt about them.

I don't believe this power to represent God's heart and feelings toward people is solely the domain of pastors—all of us are potential agents of His love and grace. That's why I want to point out this type of adult "overlooking passivity" toward children by confessing my own discovery of inadvertent neglect. Children may get used to such treatment—they may, in fact, hardly notice it. But in my view, it seems that eventually such seeds of neglect will harvest low self-esteem, whether intended or not. Inattentiveness toward people—failing to notice, to value, to acknowledge them—can introduce an undeniable depersonalizing effect. How vital it is, therefore, to make sure we don't bring this attitude to bear upon the children we pass by or contact in daily life.

After the Lord brought this problem to my awareness, I began to learn things I could do to affirm the children I met. Today, whenever I see people with kids, I will nod to the parents, greet them with a brief "Hello" and then turn my attention to the children, saying to the folks, "Excuse me just a minute." Then I take time with the kids first, often stooping low to gain a face-to-face contact with them, asking how they are, commenting positively on something they are wearing, how nice they look—saying something to the effect of "What a sharp kid you are!"

Ever since I've begun doing this, two incredible things have occurred. First, it's amazing to see how surprised many children are to realize they are taken seriously by an adult—especially one whom they know is significant in their parents' structure of things. Sometimes they don't know how to respond because it happens to them so infrequently. So it's important to learn never to be taken aback by children's bashfulness or even their seeming rejection of your greeting them. Their reaction (or lack of one) is not a reflection on you but rather on their not having had a chance to learn how to respond.

Second, it's amazing to witness, as time goes by, the anticipation on a child's face when he or she sees me coming. As children learn of an adult's interest in them and see that they are important, they blossom. The bright eyes and the smile of welcome are signs of their learning something of their own worth, even though they don't realize what is taking place in their minds and emotions.

Honor is a two-way street. To teach our children to honor their parents and to respect adults, it is important to cultivate in them a sense of their own worth as well.

Consequences of Neglecting the "Promise" Commandment

Early in the Old Testament book of 1 Kings, the biblical account of how King David raised his son Adonijah appears as a biblical paradigm filled with warning signals. It is a classic illustration of how not to parent—a dramatic story that reveals the folly of trying to please a child's whims and supposing that their character will shape itself in a positive way with the parent's misguided show of "love." Before we even get three chapters into the book, Prince Adonijah is dead by reason of his own presumption and arrogance. He is a case study of a child-become-adult who completely misses what might have been because—raised in a vacuum of unwise, nondisciplining counsel by his parents—he pursues life on his own indulgent terms, to his destruction. The short summary of the whole disaster is captured in these few words:

> Then Adonijah the son of Haggith exalted himself, saying, "*I will be king*"; and he prepared for himself chariots and horsemen, and fifty men to run before him. (And his father had not rebuked him at any time by saying, "Why have you done so?" He was also very good-looking. His mother had borne him after Absalom) (1 Kings 1:5-6, emphasis added).

Adonijah wanted to be king. The literal translation of the Hebrew is a heady proclamation: "I am going to reign!" These are not the words of a prince anticipating a future passing of the scepter to his hands; it is the cry of a brat declaring "I'm taking charge of things my way and in my time—right now!"

The background to all this should be noted: Haggith had borne David four sons, of which Adonijah was the second, Absalom being the firstborn. In sequence, it is interesting to see how both brothers tried to usurp the throne of their father at different times, and both came to similar ends. We are not told what role Haggith may have had in influencing their presumption, but it is no coincidence that her first two sons made the same devastating error. Haggith most certainly had done something in her mothering that gave place to the monstrous selfishness that brought eventual ruin to two gifted boys. However, the words of Scripture are pointed, fingering David himself as anything but blameless in what took place. That it speaks so clearly, noting how his permissiveness and unwillingness to discipline his sons gave place to the course they ultimately took, provides us with a guideline in contrast for our learning. "Look what happened: Don't raise kids this way" is clearly the lesson of the Scriptures in these episodes.

Understanding is served when we cut to the core of why such human selfishness and self-seeking are so common, why kids will—even in infancy—throw tantrums to indicate their self-will and their displeasure with anything that doesn't suit them. Of course, the sin nature of fallen man is the reason, but there is more to understanding than simply naming the sinner.

At the root of human self-seeking is the fact that there is an intuitive awareness that each of us was created to *be someone*—someone of meaning, of purpose, of "kingliness," if you will. This is because the image of God's own person—King of the universe—is upon us. However damaged or misguided by reason of sin, there is nonetheless a quest and a desire for significance within every person. This produces an inward drive to become—a drive that reveals itself in endlessly different ways in different people. The desire itself isn't really the problem; the problem is the way in which that desire is polluted and corrupted by the values of the world and pursued in the world-spirit.

> *At the root of human self-seeking there is an intuitive awareness that each of us was created to be someone of meaning, of purpose.*

Human nature that is not transformed by God's love and grace will often find itself driven to "become" at all costs and with little concern over what detriment or harm this causes others. It starts early, with the tantrum-

throwing child, the whining, the self-pitying, the screaming insistence of "I want what I want when I want it!" It is
only via responsible training, given by parents who love
enough to deny fledgling flesh and who dare to discipline
in God's firm but gracious ways, that a child can be rescued from self-destruction and away from the pollution
of the world's values.

Shepherding Through Discipline

The root of Adonijah's failure is that "his father had not
rebuked him at any time." While Adonijah was preparing
chariots and horsemen, his father, David, said nothing.
Adonijah had grown into a selfish, self-absorbed person,
consumed by his desire to rule at the expense of all else.
To say the least, he was spoiled.

Our society today thinks nothing of overindulging
children without regard to the long-term consequences.
Yet the Bible instructs us to use "the rod" (Prov. 22:15) in
order to confront such selfishness in our children. A
politically correct society shudders at the talk of such
biblical discipline. But the rod is more correctly the shepherd's rod, an instrument of guidance and protection.
The biblical rod is not an instrument of beating; it is not
the brutality depicted by Hollywood in story lines that

take religious fanatics and make their child abuse appear to be the definition of what the Bible says. Bad attitudes and behavior are not beaten out of children but confronted with correction and discipline. Sometimes the discomfort of a series of firm, stinging swats on the rump are needed to get the child's serious attention. But swats without teaching, and discipline without love are pointless exercises. True parenting shepherds children away from a path that is destructive and hell-bent and toward the path that leads to genuine fulfillment, satisfaction and happiness.

Scripture says that David never rebuked his son Adonijah. It is interesting to note that the Hebrew word for "rebuked" is cognate to a root that contains the idea of being formed, shaped or carved—as in sculpting something from stone or artistically shaping something in wood. In other words, David never bothered to shape his son. Instead, he allowed Adonijah to be shaped by circumstances—by whatever of the world's values he picked up along the way. (It is worthwhile to note that the words appearing in other Bible versions translate the word for "rebuked" as "reprimanded," "corrected," "disciplined," "displeased," "pained," "crossed," "interfered," "repressed," "restrained" or "checked"—a horrible list of things David failed to do with Adonijah.)

When parents fail to shape their children in a biblically wise way, those children may fall prey to an ugly, self-centered, self-willed, self-indulgent pursuit of life. It may at first seem relatively innocent—even "cute"—but given time may well manifest in ways that become disgusting, if not injurious, to others and end in becoming woefully abhorrent to the parents. Having not been "carved" earlier, an unshaped child becomes a misshapen teenager. By then it is often too late to exert a parental ability to guide or correct.

The Bible teaches us that we should discipline our children—that we should love them, serve them, help them to become all God intends them to be. Just as David with his son Adonijah, the failure to wisely correct and boldly shape our children can lead eventually to a self-imposed, disastrous result. Even if the disaster is unnoticeable in the sense of the grotesquely painful, there are multitudinous ways in which the tragic may still become evident. And even if physical life is not shortened, there are other ways that the beauty of life—the vitality in a relationship—may be lost, a person's destiny fall short or the joy of life as originally intended become withered.

Longevity is not only in number of years, and blessing is not only in the quantity of one's holdings. The long life and prosperity God promises to those who honor their parents come packaged more as life's fulfillments—and there is nothing more blessed than that.

Godly Advice Comes with a Blessing

Blessed is the man who walks not in the counsel of the ungodly.
PSALM 1:1

This promise of blessing goes unheeded by many in the Body of Christ today. Despite the blessing the Lord offers if we do not walk in the counsel of the ungodly, it seems that as many Christian parents are raising their kids according to the advice of secular books, magazines and TV talk shows as are raising them according to the Word of God. The values of our humanistic culture deem it socially unacceptable to reprimand, repress, restrain or discipline children. Society calls it a violation of the child's freedom and self-expression.

Simply exercising authority over a child is far from the complete picture of how discipline works. There must be equal amounts of love, service, patience, understanding and instruction. I appeal to every person who reads this book to grasp the message that God wants to plant in your heart: You can be a tremendous force for good, both to your own children and to other children under your influence. You can help them to arrive at their intended destiny. In all your relationships with children, consider that they depend upon adults as role models for how to live.

Since David never sought to shape his son, Adonijah set about shaping his own destiny. Consumed by the desire for what he wanted, he so lost his way that he even attempted to manipulate God. Instead of offering a sacrifice acceptable to the Lord in the Tabernacle, where the glory of the Lord dwelt, he offered it at a location near where Canaanite cults had practiced rituals of child sacrifice. He even invited those from his father's inner circle in the vain hope of gaining enough support to usurp his father's throne.

All of this serves to show us, not so much what a spectacular failure Adonijah was, but the tragic penalties for everyone involved when a household does not abide by God's directives for appropriate child rearing. David did not observe God's ways in raising his son, and both he and his son reaped the consequences of failing to observe God's "promise" commandment.

At the time of Adonijah's uprising, David was in his later years—a time when one might be more vulnerable to the human tendency to defer parental responsibility or even to neglect it altogether. But whatever our age—the older parent, the grandparent or the youthful parent who thinks, *C'mon, I don't feel up to this; I'm not much more than a kid myself!*—we are all assigned the responsibility to shape our kids. And always remember: That responsibility is not measured by our relative sense of preparedness, experience or present energy level. It is a measured call of God. It may seem easier not to confront ungodly attitudes and the behavior we see beginning to rise up in our children. And it may seem overblown to some to attempt to teach and lead in such a way that they learn to honor us. But Jesus has designated us as influencers and shapers of children for God's glory, not our own. God's Word has laid out the results that our influence can have—for better or for worse.

Be a blessing to the children around you by being a godly role model. Focus on affirming them and building a platform of trust by simply showing them how much you love them. The opportunity will come to give them spiritual input and guidance, and with the "weight" of honor they sense toward you, they will become receptive to the blessing you offer and receive the glorious promise of living according to God's commandments.

Prayer

Father God, help me to shape the children under my influence by loving them according to Your commandments and teaching them Your ways. I desire to be a faithful shepherd who wisely uses the rod of Your leading and correction. Teach me never to neglect or ignore any child that You bring into my life. Confront in me any harmful attitudes that linger from my own childhood. Fill me daily with Your Holy Spirit, and keep the fountain of my soul overflowing with Your wisdom, goodness and affirmation toward children so that they may become the godly nurturers and leaders of tomorrow. In Jesus' name. Amen.

Chapter Three

HUMBLE YOURSELF
AS A CHILD

At that time the disciples came to Jesus, saying, "Who then
is greatest in the kingdom of heaven?"
Then Jesus called a little child to Him, set him in the midst of
them, and said, "Assuredly, I say to you, unless you are converted
and become as little children, you will by no means enter the
kingdom of heaven. Therefore, whoever humbles himself as this
little child is the greatest in the kingdom of heaven."

MATTHEW 18:1-4

There is a freshness—an untainted beauty of possibility—
that is manifestly present in a child. The babe in arms has

more than encoded DNA in its cells that will unfold genetic data and bring about the development of every physical feature he or she will have, as well as other personal aspects of individuality. Somewhere invisibly located within heaven's rich purposes, there is a plan specifically designed by God for that life. It is not a prepackaged, irresistible arrangement of events fashioned in heaven to be imposed on the individual but a pre-planned, broad-ranging set of purposes and provisions, waiting to enable, bless and fulfill that person.

Become like a Child

Because of children's vulnerability to both the human and spiritual influences that can so easily intrude upon or damage the wonder and beauty of the heavenly Father's potential in them, Jesus taught and demonstrated a special sensitivity to these little ones. He also pressed the issue of adults coming to terms with childlikeness—clearly encouraging us to avoid the human tendencies toward hardness of heart, brittleness of soul or spiritual presumption. It is from that perspective we now turn to a passage where Jesus issued a pointed call to all Christian adults. It is a call to return to the simplicity of a child—a call that requires both rebirth and recovery.

How many of us have photos of ourselves as children that evoke disquieting memories? Maybe we've lost or thrown the photographs away, but we all have pictures in our minds that remind us of the little child we once were. My favorite picture of myself when I was a little boy is the one where I'm standing by my father's car and wearing a kind of military outfit. I was just a little kid at the time. In fact, the picture is so old that it shows me standing with my hand on the door handle and my foot up on the running board. (Somebody has to be asking "What's a running board?")

That picture brings back happy memories—first, because I really liked that outfit. (I would have called it "cool" if that colloquialism had been current then.) But the picture also shows the hills beyond our yard and brings back, even now, the smell of flowers that sprang up with springtime splendor on the hillside sloping upward to a distant peak a half-mile away. I also remember that it was the year my sister was born—how excited I was to become a big brother—and I remember it was the same year that God spared my life.

Our house was situated next to a large grove of huge eucalyptus trees. When a vicious windstorm struck our area one night, one of those trees crashed down on the house. Only because it landed at the one point where the structural capacity of the building could bear the shock and the weight was the tree kept from smashing down exactly where I was sleeping! But for God's providential grace, I probably would have been killed—one foot to either the left or right of where the tree fell would have made the difference.

Yes, that picture of a little boy still speaks—but a regained picture of any one of us will do the same. How many of us would do well to answer a dual call to be a child again—not only the call to transformation but to humble gratitude! My story of being spared is everyone's story. Only the particulars are different in regard to setting, circumstance and causal forces, yet the end result is the same. God saved my life—and He saved yours. I would like to assert this with authority: Whoever you are and no matter how much or how little anybody ever loved you, God has kept you for His own wonderful reasons—

Our heavenly Father is a faithful, loving parent whose desire is to see each of us open to receive the possibility of all that He wants to fulfill in our lives.

including the possibilities of your influence on the children in your life who have such great purpose awaiting them in His plan.

God's Word reveals that our heavenly Father is a faithful, loving parent whose desire is to see each of us open to receiving the possibility of all that He wants to fulfill in our lives. The psalmist wrote,

> How precious also are Your thoughts to me, O God!
> How great is the sum of them! (Ps. 139:17).

Once we've been converted and we recognize the depth of love the Father God has for us, we begin to be positioned— attitudinally, spiritually, pragmatically—to be instruments of blessing to our children. Fundamental to becoming effective in that way is to answer Jesus' call to become like them—truly, biblically childlike.

Be the Greatest in the Kingdom of Heaven

The broader setting for the words Jesus spoke about becoming childlike comes well into His ministry. The Twelve, who were destined for apostleship, as well as others who were following Him as disciples, had witnessed everything of God's power being manifest, including remarkable healings, awesome miracles and explosive displays of divine power that broke the chains of demonic bondage. Whether

Jesus was teaching or ministering healing, giving sight to the blind or instructing on how to reconcile relationships, His followers would hear Him say words to the effect, "The kingdom of God is in your midst." His explanation for the mightiness manifest was that God's power and rule were at work—it was "Kingdom come" in a very real way.

Gradually, Jesus' followers came to realize that His goal for them was that the same compassion, authority and power they saw revealed in His own life be manifest and ministered through theirs. However, their question, "Who then is greatest in the kingdom?" (Matt. 18:1), indicated the fundamental problem of that competitiveness born of fallen man's inbred insecurity and, thereby, a quest for more than being positioned in God's grace—a thirst for being positioned over others. Jesus set about fixing a graphic photographic image in their minds—a picture they would never forget of exactly how Kingdom power really works.

> *Jesus revealed that the entry point to God's kingdom is found in the greatness of humility, dependence and the simple trust of a child.*

His response to their question must have surprised them. Rather than instructing them on gaining dominance in their own self-interest, Jesus taught His disciples that the secret to experiencing the kingdom of God in their lives and practices was to become as a child. Think of it: Everything connected to seeing a reinstatement of God's rule in our hearts, our homes, our relationships—everything related to our gaining victory over the powers of darkness or to touching human bodies with healing graces—would require becoming a child again. Thus, Jesus revealed that the entry point to God's kingdom is found in the greatness of humility, dependence and the simple trust of a child. The master was categorical about how that happens: "Assuredly I say to you, unless you are converted" (v. 3). With the word "unless," Jesus cut out every other course. He was saying "This is the only way."

Be Converted and Become as Little Children

The word "converted" is best understood by the word "turn." "Converted" contains at least three ideas: to turn around, to turn away and to turn into. Each of these concepts is contained within the Greek verb used in this verse.

- To *turn away* is to repent. It describes the process of going in one direction and then turning around to go in the opposite direction.

- To *turn from* is to renounce, to say "I will have nothing more to do with that."
- To *turn into* is to walk through a doorway that leads into a new realm or order of things.

If we put all three elements together, we find the essence of Jesus' message to us. In order to "become as little children," we must repent, renounce the past and then find a release for the new direction that He has for us. The word "converted" contains all of this—the process that sets in motion and sustains ongoing changes in the basic structure of our lives, our thoughts and the way we respond to things. Jesus wasn't saying that we need to improve our lifestyle, clean up our act or become nicer people. He was saying that something has to happen on the inside—and He was addressing every one of us, giving us a lifelong program as His disciples. Don't miss that, because if we only see this summons of the Savior as the same as the call "You must be born again" (John 3:7), we will apply it only to evangelism— to an initial decision for Christ that results in our salvation. Jesus was talking here to disciples (already believers) and talking about a process required for effectiveness and advancement in God's purpose for believers—each and every one.

All of this is dynamically related to our capacity to bless our children. To become converted to childlikeness will transform our approach to all of life and significantly impact how we think about and relate to everyone, including our kids. It will soften and sensitize our souls; but given the fact that this renewal is happening to us as adults, a renewed view of life and ourselves under God's plan and purpose will increase our sense of significance under His design.

When thinking of Jesus' words about becoming as a little child, I often pause to think of adults who may be struggling to believe that their lives really count for all that much anymore, especially if they have passed into the middle years. The whole structure of our society argues that worth is wrapped up in youthfulness. Consequently, we are pressed or tempted to struggle to verify that we have retained something of that. Yet there is a vast difference between aging and gaining maturity. Aging is something the body does. Maturity happens to the human character.

> *Aging is something the body does; maturity happens to the human character.*

To those who say to themselves, *My life is pretty much over and done; I may still have some years to live out, but what consequence do they have?* hear Jesus saying to you, "I want you to become as a little child again." He's talking about a renewal of His creative power in your life, about a reinstating of the richness of the Father's lifetime purpose for you—getting you in gear again! He can begin something new and fulfilling in you that's never happened before, something you will be able to "will" to your spiritual heirs—the children you bless.

Define the Child We Are to Become

It is significant to understand the definition of the word "child" as Jesus used it in this passage. There are a number of terms used to refer to children that describe different stages of development and maturity, so there are a number of Greek words used in the Scriptures for "child." There are specific words such as *huios* and *thugater,* which mean "son" and "daughter," respecively. Further, there are more general words for children such as *napia, paidia* and *teknoi,* which, respectively, refer to "infants," "growing children" and "children in general." The word Jesus chose to use in this particular instance was "paidia"—growing children.

I remember a recent occasion when Anna and I tried to organize a family photograph. It was one of the rare times when we were able to coordinate having all of our children and grandchildren together at our house at the same time (a remarkable challenge with our kids' families in three different states and grandkids spanning ages 1 to 20). It was an absolutely hilarious spectacle. We had hired a photographer, but in hindsight we should have gotten a Hollywood producer with motion picture or video cameras.

Now, I want to say with genuine truthfulness and not merely grandparental pride that all our grandchildren are good kids, but this event was nothing short of a study in perpetual motion. As soon as one child was settled, another would squirm or wiggle. (Growing children are always on the move!) It was a miracle that out of the 20 photos taken by the photographer ("Everybody look this way . . . smile . . . look here, Carl [the baby] . . . uh, the little girl on the left, closer to your brother . . ." etc., etc.), there was just one that was good. That adventure makes me wonder what it seems like to our heavenly Father as He seeks to help us get the picture of His purpose in us and form the image of Jesus in our character.

Reflect the Three Childlike Qualities

Each person who opens up to God's love in His Son, Jesus, is described in God's Word as having been "born of the Spirit" (John 3:6), as "a new creature in Christ" (see 2 Cor.

5:17). As His babes in arms to begin with, we have come into the family of a loving Father who wants to bring us forward in growth, understanding and character to a realization of His purpose and potential for us. With the footing of this understanding, we can see how the definitions above apply as we learn to grow and be taught. First, irrespective of our point of growth, we are the Father's teknoi—His in the generic sense—all sons and daughters of God. But second, in the text we're discussing, Jesus is saying that He wants us to become paidioi—"grown up" enough to become children of that degree of maturity that we may be shaped in childlikeness by Him. To grasp this, let us look at three basic qualities that sum up the childlikeness God wants us to possess: expectancy, humility and teachability.

Become Expectant as a Child

Few things are as beautiful as looking into the bright eyes of a child anticipating a Christmas morning. Expectations run high for a basic reason: Children who know they are loved are sure there will be loving gifts provided for them. This simple analogy needs to ply the edges of my soul— and yours too. As we walk with God over accumulating years, He will regularly call us to fresh expectations. He has not ordained life as a dull routine but as an adventure.

But only the soul that is learning to rest in His love will live with a divinely intended expectancy that sees each new day as an opportunity to discover God's good purpose and opportunities to serve Him joyfully.

From my own experience, I can say that the longer I walk with the Lord, the more He surprises me. Each surprise calls me to new dimensions of trust, because few of these adventures are either convenient or without the requirement of new dimensions of growth. How easy to tell oneself, *I've "grown up" in God—I'm mature enough.* Not that any of us would willingly arrogate such a proposition, but how many might shrink back from opening to another step of trust because the Holy Spirit is prompting a new expectancy? If I yield to that reticence—give place to that loss of expectancy—then I have fallen into the trap of true aging, which is simply the result of allowing my soul to grow old. But true childlikeness is that maturity that never loses an available readiness to expect, to be open to God regularly doing something new in our lives.

Become Humble as a Child

I've often watched the kids at our church—how they gather with their Sunday School teachers and enter into worship and singing—and I am touched by the unaffected humility and lack of self-consciousness in their attitude.

At least until near-teen years arrive, their responses in worship are profoundly open. If the teacher encourages them to clap their hands joyfully or raise them reverently, every child in the room enters in with simplicity and willingness. Small hands are raised and heads are lifted heavenward. No wonder "their angels always see the face of My Father" (Matt. 18:10). Adult inclinations to social sophistication or pride would find a thousand reasons to resist such openness; but childlike humility enters—and that's what Jesus meant about this aspect of entering the kingdom of God. He wasn't referencing heaven—someday, somewhere—but entering the dimensions of God's presence and power now!

Become Teachable as a Child

With expectancy via trusting faith, and humility before God with a pride-rejecting commitment, we will find lesson upon lesson offered to us by the Holy Spirit's work in our lives. These lessons are usually life experiences, not Bible studies. As important as our study of God's Word is, it is only when it becomes integrated into an expectant, humble and loving lifestyle that we have truly answered to the childlike trait of teachability. Growth doesn't take place through the acquisition of information but by applying the information we receive.

Jesus summons us to allow these principles to work in our lives if we are going to be a blessing to our children. Our challenge, as parents, is to tune in—to listen to the Holy Spirit speaking through God's Word—to hear what He is saying to us. That necessity prompts a memory, perhaps instructively illustrative.

Until a few years ago, I had sporadic, recurrent earaches most of my life—not intense or debilitating, but aggravating, short-term discomfort—and often attended by a stuffiness that blocked or seriously inhibited my hearing. As the result of an inquiry I made of my doctor when I was having my annual physical examination, I came to realize I need never have endured those earaches at all. He diagnosed how my ears produced wax at a faster than average rate, which resulted in pain and intermittent loss of hearing. Learning how to soften the wax inside my ears with oil and remove it with cotton was a simple solution to a frustrating and painful problem I thought I would have to live with for the remainder of my years.

It shortly occurred to me that the increased clarity in my hearing and the removal of cyclic occurrences of pain all had to do with learning how to maintain my hearing apparatus. The key was in the softening effect of the oil—and what a profound parallel this represents. It is so like our need to hear the Savior's call to listen and learn. How easily the soul's ears can "age" and thereby bring an accumulated waxiness of fleshly production that inevitably brings limited hearing (or responsiveness) and eventual pain (in us or others). The answer is still in the oil! This great symbol of the Holy Spirit points to that aspect of our adult thought and lifestyle most vulnerable to hardening—our hearts. But at the bottom line, the hardening of our soul's arteries is nothing more than an unwillingness (or unavailability) to listen and to learn like a child.

Jesus is calling each of us who would bless a child to become one.

Yes, Jesus is calling each of us who would bless a child to become one. It's a becoming-converted process of turning toward—of never forgetting that, however much we mature, we're still always children before our heavenly Father.

And learning that will increase our ministry to the children He gives us to influence by our ever-growing lives.

Prayer

Dear Lord, anoint my ears to hear even the faintest whisper of Your Holy Spirit, and soften my heart to be receptive and pliable to Your Word. Let my hands become instruments of Your blessing. Make me as vulnerable to Your Spirit as a child to his parents, and use the children in my life to recover in me the open trust and joyfulness that You intended for all of us who are called Your sons and daughters. I humble myself before You in asking these things, in the name of my Lord and Savior, Jesus Christ. Amen.

Chapter Four

WHAT HAPPENS WHEN WE DON'T BLESS OUR CHILDREN

Whoever receives one little child like this in My name receives Me.

MATTHEW 18:5

Following the change Jesus calls for in us—that we be converted and become as little children—He issues the above charge of responsibility: *Receive a little child.* Children are at the mercy of the shaping influences around them. If their personalities are established without wisdom, love and acceptance, then it is certain they will carry forward into their adult lives a degree of bondage—that weighty package the sin of neglect or violation leaves behind. Even if children come from happy homes, it is the fallen-sin nature of man that passes the inheritance of brokenness—in one form or another—to the children. Jesus is concerned that we properly steward and bless our children, so they may grow up to become transparent, confident adults capable of transmitting that blessing to the next generation.

Receive a Child, Like Jesus Did

Take heed that you do not despise one of these little ones,
for I say to you that in heaven their angels always see the
face of My Father who is in heaven.

MATTHEW 18:10

Most of us reading the words "do not despise one of these little ones" would doubtless think to ourselves, *I would never despise a child.* But the setting of Jesus' exhortation is not to a band of child abusers; He was speaking with disciples. So what did Jesus mean?

The common association we make with the word "despise" would be characterized by feelings of contempt, animosity or hatred. But in the New Testament text, the same word used here occurs in 1 Thessalonians 5:20, which cautions us with the warning, "Do not despise prophecies." Through this context—which refers to the various ways people treat prophetic "words" of edification, exhortation or comfort given through the Holy Spirit's gift of prophecy (see 1 Cor. 14:4)—we might gain a clearer perspective on our vulnerability to "despising" a child and hardly being aware of it. Let's look at some ways that might happen:

- Prophetic words are silenced by people who disallow them to be spoken.
- Prophetic words are exploited or twisted to serve other than their intended purpose in God's will.
- Prophetic words are trivialized by failure to consider the depth inherent in their apparent simplicity.
- Prophetic words are given or delivered, but nothing whatsoever is said or done about the words spoken.

It doesn't require much to see how each of these ways devalues a "present word" from God and to see as well a parallel in the ways that adults may too easily disregard the presence of God in a child and thereby "despise" him or her.

- Children are sometimes silenced in ways that are other than simply corrective.
- Children are sometimes exploited to serve selfish adult agendas.
- Children are sometimes trivialized by adult insensitivity to the deeper wells within them.
- Children are sometimes ignored or overlooked, even when crying for attention.

This order of despising may come in so many ways—casually, indifferently, passively or with active malice—but the majority of times it will not likely be the latter. We need to see each child as an incarnate statement of God, a "word" waiting to be received, understood, aligned with God's eternal Word and actuated to the Holy Spirit's intended purpose. To do otherwise is to fail to heed Jesus' warning, "Don't despise a child," a warning that issues an imperative: *You cannot do that with kids, not if you are My disciple.*

Be Stewards of Children

Children are present in everyone's life—whether in close proximity or distant, whether tykes or teens, whether the interaction is anticipated or not or whether the child is a relative or not. Children are placed into our stewardship in a variety of ways. If you have children in your home—whether they were born to you, adopted by you or placed in your charge for some other reason—it is obvious where your spiritual stewardship begins. But what if you aren't a parent or don't have kids living in your home? Maybe you have nieces or nephews; perhaps you've watched your best friends start their families and you love their kids as if they were yours. These are the children in your immediate circle.

Then again, perhaps you're a parent whose children have grown up and moved out. If that's the case, maybe you think you've already done your part. Anna and I learned that even when our kids had left home, they were never really gone—not because they were back knocking on the door, begging for a handout, but because we hold a lifetime bond in our hearts for our children, an inescapable "presence" that often brings them to mind. The responsibility we feel for them is never over. As a matter of fact, it keeps multiplying because, eventually, the grandchildren arrive—and maybe even great-grandchildren!

Add to this the little boy next door or the girl across the street, the children we meet in passing or the kids in our church—how can blessing be ministered to them? The stewardship of our power to bless might come in the form of working in the nursery or teaching a Sunday School class. It might come by volunteering to bring a smile to the faces of kids who are sick in the hospital or becoming a Big Brother or Big Sister to a child who has no viable parents but just needs to know that he or she is valued. You and I have a marvelous potential for planting self-esteem into children— for ministering God's love in ways that stick for a lifetime—and it's not about lecturing them but about loving them.

You and I have a marvelous potential for planting self-esteem into children—for ministering God's love in ways that stick for a lifetime.

In the midst of such renewed sensitivity toward kids, it's imperative that we don't neglect to show the love of God to their parents as well. We can help the parents become beneficiaries of God's will and thereby initiate a heritage and legacy for them to pass on to their kids. All these things are part of the way we can answer Jesus' call that all His disciples have a part to play in receiving and blessing children.

Ponder the Moment More Fully

Join me in further thoughts regarding how Jesus received the child and brought us these lessons, pondering that memorable moment more fully. When Jesus focused His attention upon the little child, Matthew's account says He "called a little child to Him, [and] set him in the midst of them" (18:2). Mark's account says much the same thing, but it gives an added bit of information:

> Then He took a little child and set him in the midst
> of them. And when He had taken him in His arms,
> He said to them (9:36).

Jesus took the little child in His arms. Why didn't Matthew say that?

The synoptic gospels regularly offer added depth of perspective in this way—each providing a viewpoint on episodes from a different perspective. Imagine all the people gathered around Jesus, looking at Him from different angles, different aspects, and it is easy to see how the writers of the gospels have triangulated on Jesus— each reporting from their unique point of coverage of His life. What each one saw was not contradictory to what the others saw; it was supplemental. The gospels of Matthew, Mark and Luke together give us a three-dimensional view of Jesus. In this case, it is Mark who adds the distinctive fact that Jesus actually held the child in His arms as He spoke.

Some commentators have suggested that perhaps Mark remembered and included that remark because he was the child who sat on Jesus' lap. Since Mark wrote his gospel in the A.D. 50s, well over 20 years after Jesus ministered, and while Mark was still a reasonably young man at the time of his writing, this is a credible proposal. In his gospel there are one or two other references that some think to be Mark's referring to himself, though he never makes a direct statement to that effect. If the child in this passage was Mark as a young boy, then it is certainly understandable that he would remember the day Jesus held him on His lap; it is equally desirable that this would be distinctly noted. Why? Because it reflects the humanness of Jesus in a more tender way. And whether or not Mark was the child, that fact remains.

Understand How the World Suffers When Children Do

Why did Jesus actually hold the child? I believe it was to reinforce and add further weight to His words. Haven't we all, as parents, called our children over to our laps or put an arm around a teenager to tell them something special? It's a natural thing as a human being to draw children close to us when we want to share something of particular value or meaning with them—words of praise and encouragement as well as words of correction. The bond that physical contact creates says far more than our words; it says, "I love you; I receive you; I welcome and value your life as part of mine." And it's exactly the same kind of intimacy our Father God desires with us—a fact proven by the actions of His Son.

And so, with the child in His lap, as if Jesus is shielding and protecting him, the Lord then gives His people a severe and stern warning:

> Whoever causes one of these little ones who believe in Me to sin, it would be better for him if a millstone were hung around his neck, and he were drowned in the depth of the sea (Matt. 18:6).

This is an incredible illustration that makes it impossible for us to miss the importance of Jesus' words. In those days, a millstone was used for the grinding out of grain. It was housed in a circular trough, which was pulled around by a beast of burden. These millstones could be four to six feet in diameter and were approximately 18 inches thick. The weight of one millstone approached a ton, so the force of Jesus' point is dramatized when He said what he did about it being better to tie a millstone around your neck and be thrown into the sea than to lose your sensitivity toward children. How profoundly pointed!

And then Jesus continued,

> Woe to the world because of offenses! For offenses must come, but woe to that man by whom the offense comes! (Matt. 18:7).

What offenses is Jesus talking about? He's talking about the way children are violated, hurt or wounded—sadly, about things that can and do happen. He is saying that more is caused than the obvious pain inflicted upon the child or children involved. Through the mistreatment of children, something distills over all humanity with a deteriorating force. Our Creator-Savior specifically says there is a "woe"—a sorrowful, heart-wrenching impact—upon the world, a suffering under great pain because of all the offenses committed against children. Even if we limit our examination of this to our personal experience, most of us recall at some point in our childhood when we felt rejected, hurt or

Through the mistreatment of children, something distills over all humanity with a deteriorating force.

abused. The pain felt often remains to this very moment and has an awful—indeed, a woeful—capability of multiplying itself in pain upon pain.

In saying it is inevitable that the offenses come, the Lord was not being fatalistic but simply realistic. Why? Because fallen man is incapable of doing anything else. Offenses will come whether we like it or not; our call is to understand this harsh reality and seek to minister healing and to live in ways that will preempt the effect of such violation.

Jesus' use of the word "offenses," which points to the severity of the issue, is from the Greek word *scandalon,* the word from which our English word "scandal" is derived. "Scandalon" not only suggests scandalous things but goes further—referring to a trigger that springs a trap. It directly refers to the lever on which bait is put and which, when touched, drops a cage or springs a trap that maims or kills an animal.

So Jesus was speaking of woe to the world because of the things humans do that will entrap children in bondage for the rest of their lives—things that spring out of a moment's violation, temper, carelessness of speech or recklessness of attitude toward a child. Psychologically, these cumulative episodes of temper or careless speech become the trap that springs and the hooks that snap, inflicting a gash, a wound, a bruise—sometimes bringing outright death to many of that child's possibilities and prospects for effective living. While children's biological lives may be sustained, their potential has been trapped and slaughtered.

But "scandalon" goes even beyond that, containing the idea of something that repulses. In short, the offense sickens, causing one to draw back in horror and, for the rest of a child's life, to say to anything even associated with the memory of the offense, "I hate that!" or "I want nothing do with that—ever!"

Such biblical revelation calls us to help protect and steward children so that such wounds are, at the very least, radically reduced in number if not completely prevented. Our responsibility is to seek to rescue and preserve the innocence of the child. To do that effectively, we need an awareness of some of the most common things that cause offense to a child.

Avoid the Dirty Dozen

With that goal in view, and from my years of counseling adults and discovering the problems mature individuals deal with that go back to childhood offenses, I have formulated a list of 12 such offenses. I call them the dirty dozen.

1. Impacted by Neglect

Children are often wounded through the impact of neglect. The Bible says that a child left to himself brings his parents to shame (see Prov. 29:15). Sometimes children are just left alone. It's not a matter of calculated abandonment; it's just that nobody is home with them. Maybe the parents aren't around from the time the kid comes home after school until 5:30 P.M.—or later. That's not going to ruin a child for one day of his or her life, or even for one unusual week, but it definitely impacts that child if nobody's ever there.

"Well, they're pretty mature kids," someone may say. "They get along all right." So we allow ourselves to buy into society's proposition that we should live our lives to the fullest and let kids figure it out for themselves. But in so doing, what are we breeding into society? Who is discipling our children during the hours we leave them alone? Who is discipling them while they are sitting in front of the TV by themselves, watching whatever comes on?

What we are breeding is loneliness and sometimes, worse than that, exposure to the destructive or release to the irresponsible. Nobody can calculate the future cost of those dangers. But there is a second and even greater point of neglect that can have an ultimately damning influence. It's the neglect of loving discipline.

Unfortunately, even in the light of increased social studies verifying the problems caused as youthful respect for authority diminishes, there seems to be a growing neglect of teaching parents effective means of administering child discipline. Intimidated by the fear of being charged with child abuse for exercising any order of even the mildest corporal punishment, and being scoffed at times for bold, corrective punitive action, parents may be understandably hesitant but not justifiably negligent.

The "rod" is the opposite of neglect and it has nothing to do with beating, screaming, hitting, brutalizing, bullying or arguing. It is love in action.

There is a way to learn to administrate biblical discipline with children. The "rod" does not refer to a board, a whip or any implement that would cause injury. Instead, the rod refers to something more on the order of a shepherd's instrument of care—a symbol of firm government, serious instruction, careful explanation, strict lines drawn, full obedience expected and penalties measured firmly when violation takes place. It is the opposite of neglect and it has nothing to do with beating, screaming, hitting, brutalizing, bullying or arguing. It is love in action—the use of words and acts that will give the child understanding and extend meaningful care for the child's well-being and security through it all.

To neglect the parental use of the rod in this regard will breed indifference in children and end in developing people who expect to do whatever they feel or want with presumed impunity. It will spawn a generation that says, "If it feels good, do it. Forget the consequences; there are none!" And that's a lie. Neglected discipline is destructive. Buying into any philosophy that justifies it or any convenience that omits it is giving place to the same deception. (We will discuss discipline in more detail in chapter 5.)

2. Tainted by Impurity

Children are so often tainted by impurity—things they are exposed to in their innocence that bring about a shocked response within them and create a wound. The tainting that comes through impurity brings us to a number of points of accountability. It is a challenge to protect the innocence of a child in the face of the vast resources of the mass media pumped daily into our homes. I feel a special compassion for parents seeking to raise godly children today in the midst of the profusion of profane and lewd output that is abundantly available. I hope that it would be beyond any believer in Jesus Christ to invest their money in it, but you don't even have to subscribe to adult cable channels for your kids to be exposed to sexual immorality and the worst kind of values presented as normal behavior.

The real tragedy of a child whose innocence has been tainted by impurity is the readiness with which they will accept further impurity with a lesser degree of shock. Eventually it becomes a lifestyle. The child may no longer view what they see as being unusual or abnormal. And that's the heart of the problem. They are so surrounded by impurity that they cease to recognize it as impure.

There is an absence of wisdom among some parents by not protecting their children from seeing times of marital intimacy. I could tell numerous stories of instances I have dealt with where people had a fundamental revulsion for normal sexual intercourse in their own marriage because of a single instance as a child when they discovered their parents making love. These unwise—and I would go so far as to say reckless, if not ignorant—parents had not paid enough attention to preserving the privacy of their own intimacy and, inevitably, one of their children inadvertently broke in on it. Parents, it's not a matter of protecting yourselves from embarrassment; it's a matter of protecting children who do not know how to handle what they see, especially small children. They don't really understand, but they know something is going on—and that's another problem. They know something, but they don't know enough. And what they don't know creates fear, revulsion and shock.

The Bible is very pointed about the responsibility of parents to preserve their privacy—their personal physical privacy and their intimate marital privacy—from their children. Not because the Bible is prudish, but because it is wise. God knows the makeup of our personalities and how easily children are offended.

3. Demeaned by Ridicule

The third way children are offended is when their self-esteem is shredded by ridicule. "You stupid kid . . . why can't you be more like your brother?" Or "You know, you're just a constant headache." A child doesn't need to hear that very many times before he or she believes it. Self-esteem isn't generated by who we are or what we're capable of; it comes from what we think of ourselves, beginning with what's planted in us as children about life's possibilities and our sense of being able to see those hopes realized.

I once dealt with a very gifted young person who, having been raised in a family with a common, simple surname, was often told by her parent, "You can't expect to

be thought important: after all, we're only _____s"
(repeating their surname). What could have been done by
the parent was a study into the history of the family surname to see the many people of achievement who bore
that name, people who had achieved great things or made
wonderful contributions to humankind. Relating this to
children—"This is the kind of family we come from"—
would so obviously be preferable to having them see their
name—and thereby their person—as unworthy.

Because the opposite had been spoken over and over
to the young adult I was seeking to help bring to a point
of self-respect, it was easy to see why she wrestled with the
tendency to think so negatively about herself.

The child who is put down, as well as the child whose
accomplishments are not acknowledged, will have a shriv-
eled sense of self-esteem. It is why some people who seem
well equipped in natural gifts cannot seem to fulfill their
potential, while others beginning with so much less in the
way of natural gifting end up soaring to the heights of
achievement.

Dear adult friend, dear parent or grandparent, I am
not suggesting that we artificially contrive imaginary or
deluding notions and seek to sell them to kids. I am saying that we are charged to do nothing that detracts from,
demeans or diminishes a child's sense of the beauty of

God's purpose in them, His design for them or the creative power available to them.

4. Debased by Poverty

I remember talking once with a young black man, a student around 20 years old. I'll call him Michael. He was a very gifted guy with real fire in him. But I saw something in him that was taking him to the verge of destruction—an attitude I wanted to help him separate from the very clear call of God on his life. I have a particular passion to see strong black leadership rising in our culture today—especially in the Church. Outstanding male role models are needed everywhere, but something of the shabby history of the past centuries in North America has eroded the sense of manhood among many blacks. Michael was a giant waiting to happen—a guy who could be the answer to a thousand challenges if I could help him sort out what was going on inside him. The problem wasn't between us—he liked me—but Michael was loaded with hatred that found its origin in the destructive atmosphere of debasing poverty he had been dragged through as a child.

One day I invited him into the office and we began talking. I soon confronted that ragged edge in him that threatened the possibility of his real fruitfulness. As we talked, he started to get choked with anger, but he didn't know how to direct it. He said to me, "Pastor Hayford, if you only knew—" and then he began to tell me things that had happened to him and his brother as little boys—unimaginable things, from common crudity to being driven to eat out of the garbage can because of their desperate hunger.

When Michael grew up and broke away from that existence, the discovery of the social dynamics that affected his poverty—with no compassion or nurturing introduced to that setting—fostered rage. When I showed him my genuine care and belief in him and pointed to what Jesus had experienced of mistreatment and how He comes presently to help us break through and break out of that bondage, Michael's rage was overcome and the passion for life and for helping others found direction. Michael's fire needed the kind of ignition that only the Holy Spirit can bring; but a human vessel—an adult who loves and communicates with understanding and respect—can make a world of difference.

5. Violated Through Abuse

More kids than we realize have had their personalities devastated because of abuse. A young girl—I'll call her Toni—not yet 20 years old, was brought to our church by an older couple who had taken her under their wing, seeking to nourish her to healing and wholeness. Toni came from a demented background that had sent her into a life of prostitution. As a child, she was subjected to ongoing incest that was—unbelievably—approved of by the church her parents attended. Who can fathom such blindness—such evil! Having been reduced to a sex object as a child, it apparently made it acceptable for her to become a sex object for money. Out of that abuse was born a hatred for men in general and a quest to control any man who came into her life.

One day, following a church service, the couple who were helping Toni asked if I would see her for just a moment. I did, and as she shared briefly and not accusingly, she described how she had been hurt by something I had said in a sermon. "It's not really so much what you said, Pastor—my pain isn't your fault. You were simply teaching truth. But because of my past, it made me feel so unclean." She began to weep. She said, "Pastor Jack, do you think I'm unclean?"

Oh, God! I was so deeply moved! Looking directly in her eyes, I reached out and took that child in my arms—hugging her and expressing the Father's love in Jesus' name as I was on the verge of tears. Those who were with me prayed gently, surrounding the moment with divine grace. It was an overwhelmingly tender moment to see this frail, broken person—now so physically wasted through having been exploited as a prostitute—respond to the love of the team who joined me.

From there, an older couple in the church took over for several weeks, modeling and teaching Toni in the love, compassion and wisdom of God—transmitting God's spiritual blessings from generation to generation. Toni received Jesus Christ as her Lord and Savior and, over time, has been gradually recovering. She, of course, immediately received forgiveness from Jesus Christ, and soon thereafter she experienced a real deliverance through the power of the Holy Spirit. But she is still sometimes an emotional basket case. (Oh, how God abhors the offenses the world inflicts on a child!) But this child, praise God, is coming to wholeness. Hallelujah!

6. Humiliated by Authority

Children are vulnerable to those in authority over them and especially to the words spoken to them by someone they respect and admire. It might not be an intentional remark, but a teacher, coach or relative—anyone close who expresses their disapproval—can wound a child. It might be a sharp word of retort or a throwaway comment, such as "Get out of the game," hollered from the sidelines because the child fumbled the ball when it was snapped from the center. It seems understandable, given the context, and for the moment doesn't appear to be a big deal; but something destructive happens inside the child.

What about a child who doesn't often have the right answer in class? Maybe he or she is a good kid but not a real sharp student, but this particular time he or she happens to know the answer to a question the teacher is asking. The child's hand is stretching up; but the teacher passes by and moves on to another child who always gets it right, as if to say, "You dummy, we can't count on you for anything." *But I knew that answer,* the child thinks, *and I never got a chance to say it.* Even without words, humiliation and worthlessness can be perceived from the teacher's stance, glance, mood or mode of communication.

7. Bruised by Disappointment

Children can be deeply offended by disappointment and broken promises. Maybe the child was graduating from sixth grade and the parents didn't come. Maybe it was the Little League finals. Dad said he would be there, but he wasn't. Later he says, "Hey, I'm sorry. I just couldn't make it." The father is clueless that he has just let his child down and inflicted an emotional bruise upon him. Later this child becomes an adult who finds it hard to trust and have faith, or the child may also become an adult who does not keep his word.

8. Shattered by Divorce

How many offended children are there whose lives have been torn apart by divorce? One of children's most common responses to divorce is to believe it was their fault. Can you explain why this is? It doesn't seem to enter the children's minds that there's a problem between their parents. Psychiatrists and psychologists have difficulty explaining why children feel they are to blame, despite their parents telling them otherwise. When divorce occurs, it doesn't only break the bond between husband and wife, but it also rips through the fabric of the entire family. What absolute craziness it is that governs a culture that serves its own convenience and sacrifices its own commitment simply because "it's just not working for me anymore"! It's not just the marriages that are shattered; the kids are shattered too. On top of that we can add the constant competitiveness from alienated parents contending for their children's affections. The kids are torn even more.

9. Demoted by Disability

What I mean by disability isn't necessarily a handicap—just limited ability. Perhaps a child is a little slow in school or not as capable as other kids. Or maybe the kid has always been the last one to be chosen for the team when it comes time to play games. Maybe there is some absence of coordination or of intellectual quickness. That's the benchmark society uses to measure everything: how are you in academics and athletics?

A child with limited abilities isn't doomed to be demoted. We must remember this all the more when dealing with special-needs children. Children wounded because they don't "measure up" lose the possibility of finding their true potential fulfilled, and the world loses out on receiving what they might have contributed. Woe to the world because of offenses!

10. Poisoned by Pornography

When I was a boy of just eight years old, I visited a friend's house where his 13-year-old brother handed me a sheet of paper. Eight-year-old Jack Hayford leaned over to read that sheet, and as I began to read, every flame that could be turned on inside a relatively innocent little kid who knew very little about sex—certainly in the way it was being represented on that page—was turned on. I did not become overwhelmed by the fire of arousal, because there was some maturity in me that understood this kind of sexual exercise. But I didn't understand until years later that the real impact was a spirit of pornography that, like a giant leech, had attached itself to me. Though I never spent any money on pornography, and though all this preceded today's era of ready availability via the Internet, I struggled with temptation in this regard. For years I could not understand why I constantly wrestled foul thoughts in my mind, until in my adult years the Holy Spirit traced the way back to that day as an eight-year-old and I allowed Him to heal me from it.

Only recently I talked to a brokenhearted young man who was dealing with a devastating trial in his family situation. He cited an instance when one day he went into his father's closet to look innocently for something and found his dad's stash of pornographic magazines. He was badly affected, not only by what he saw in the magazines, but also by how finding them changed his view of his dad whom he so highly respected.

11. Battered by Brutality

Some children have been unimaginably brutalized by a parent or someone else who is an authority figure. Being constantly beaten causes loss of security, loss of a capacity for gentleness and the loss of a sense of self-confidence. What happens when a person's spirit is downcast and broken this way? The Bible says that "a broken spirit dries the bones" (Prov. 17:22). In this poetic reference to the bones, a prophetic picture is cast that relates to human anatomy. Our bones are the source that feeds our blood system, which in turn feeds our flesh. Thus the Bible is saying that when a person's spirit has been broken, then even the very sap of life that runs through them and gives them their sense of person and meaning is being devastated. Even if a child who has been subjected to physical brutality rises above being visibly or attitudinally downcast, the opposite may appear: There can come a deep, tooth-clenching defiance against everybody and everything. In either case, brutality registers its destructive impact.

12. Mocked for Their Appearance

The last of this dirty dozen is the offense children suffer as a result of being mocked for their appearance. As adults, we know that the 11-year-old kid with the gangly walk or the 7-year-old with the uncomely face can turn out to be the most graceful, the loveliest or the most handsome of the college sophomore class. But it's often too late by then. The offense has been registered. No matter how they look later, most will regard themselves on the basis of remarks that were made back when their personalities were being formed.

Ideally, parents would be sensitive to the vulnerability of their children, but they are not always. There is the guy who is a bit slow to grow, so he's jokingly called "the runt." There's the girl who is tall for her age, so she's called "beanpole." Our culture and media contribute their damage by presenting unrealistic or even negative images of what constitutes attractiveness.

Sensitivity to each of the above points must become an acquired way of thinking and an ongoing lifestyle if we are going to bless our children. When Jesus said, "Woe to the world because of offenses," He wasn't only talking about the offense that the child—and the offender—endure. He was also warning of what the world loses when a broken child is unable to fulfill or contribute what he or she was created to be and do. Also included in that warning is the damage our world endures when the offended child becomes a bitter and angry adult who passes down a broken legacy from generation to generation.

There is a generation of children all around us—across the street, around our neighborhood, throughout our city. The Lord has said that He wants us to take stewardship for those children. Disciples do that—they don't just get changed, they accept a charge. Jesus is calling a people who will be born into His kingdom. He is calling them to be transformed in their beings as they become childlike in their faith and humility, liberated in their worship, expectant, teachable and ministering to others. They will go on to impact the lives of the generation emerging around them and break the cycle of offense that so damages the world and its people. He's calling us to be stewards of His children.

Each child and every child is very, very precious. Jesus pressed this point in His parable of the one lost sheep (see Matt. 18:12-13). In the final analysis, the blessing of our children, by carefully avoiding or ministering to the aftermath of those things that bring brokenness instead of blessing, will ultimately mean their salvation. What is the value of one sheep? Jesus answered that question for us. God calls us to place a high value on children, to seek to preserve them from as much of this world's damaging impact as possible and bring them early to know Jesus as Savior. He stresses in His Word that we should nurture our children, because if they can be brought to salvation at an early age, they will be rescued from many things that would seek to hurt, destroy or ruin their lives.

> *There is a generation of children all around us, and the Lord wants us to take stewardship for those children.*

When the great preacher Dwight L. Moody returned from an evangelistic service at a local church one evening, a friend asked, "Reverend Moody, were there any converts tonight?"

The renowned evangelist paused a moment, enumerating the results, and then replied, "Yes, there were three and one-half."

To this, the friend responded, "Ah, three adults and a child."

But Moody replied, "No, there were three children and an adult." He then continued, answering the bewildered look on the inquirer's face. "An adult only has half a life remaining to live for Christ, but the children will have the entirety of their lives to know His blessing and serve His will."

Answering the call to bless our children ultimately answers the call to see entire lifetimes come to know and experience eternal blessings—beginning now, throughout life and on into eternity.

A Prayer for Those Who Need Healing

Lord Jesus, I open my heart and let You into places of hurt and shame I may never have opened to anyone else before. I surrender my anger and bitterness and submit to Your process of deliverance. Take from me

*now those snares that have been planted by the enemy
of my soul and replace them with the loving fellowship
of Your comforter, the Holy Spirit, who drives away all
my fear. I praise Your holy name, Lord God! I rejoice
at Your goodness and mercy. I forgive completely all
who have wounded me and release them to Your abun-
dant blessing that they too might be converted into children of the Kingdom. Thank You for the overflow of
Your healing and grace. I worship You with all my
heart, dear Lord. In Jesus' name I pray. Amen.*

A Prayer to Ask for Forgiveness

*Lord, I come to You to ask Your forgiveness where I
have been guilty of offending others and where I have
hurt people without even knowing it. If there is restitu-
tion You would have me make, or people whose forgiveness I need to ask, bring that discernment clearly to me
now and open the door for healing between us. Let the
grace and mercy You show to me now be multiplied
upon those whom I have wounded, mistreated, over-
looked or failed to defend. Teach me to walk in a path
of righteousness for Your sake. Cleanse me of all
unrighteousness, and fill my heart with Your peace. In
Jesus' name I pray. Amen.*

A Prayer to Accept the Charge of Stewardship

Heavenly Father, in Jesus' name, I give You all the praise and honor. I am Your servant. I accept the responsibility of stewardship for Your little ones. Let the words of Jesus become incarnate in my life that I may be a faithful disciple who receives the child and stewards a generation against damaging offenses. Anoint my tongue. Bless me with compassion, wisdom, discernment and resources to find and protect Your lost lambs and to minister the life and glory of Jesus Christ to Your innocent babes. Amen.

Chapter Five

LEARNING GOD'S WAY OF CORRECTION

For as the heavens are higher than the earth,
so are My ways higher than your ways.

ISAIAH 55:9

There is nothing more precious than the gift of life, noth-ing more delicate to be preserved and protected than the life and well-being of a child. If there is anything the Bible defends, it is life. The entirety of God's loving plan of salvation is intended that none should perish (see 2 Pet. 3:9) and, in giving His own life for humankind, Jesus made the ultimate statement as to God's opinion about the preciousness of each human being (see John 3:16).

That is why it is absolutely mystifying that anyone would ever distort the biblical directives on the disciplining of children as potentially destructive. It is so regrettable that anyone has ever taken direct quotes from the Bible—that is, out of their true, whole-Bible context—and used them to justify abusive treatment. Worse, when such unthinkable violations make the news in court cases of brutalized or emotionally abused children, the same half-truth quotations are aired to millions of television viewers in tandem with pictures of children's bruised bodies. And the abusive adult's appearance seems almost always to justify the evidence that they are in possession of a less-than-sound mind. Taken all together, the sum of it seems to establish something of a public notion that "child discipline" on the lips of a believer in the Bible is presumed to justify cruel, cold-blooded treatment of children in the name of God.

Understanding Biblical Discipline

Given this challenge to clear communication, one would be inclined to simply bypass the subject of disciplining a child and thereby bypass the risk of being thought other than sensible, humane or in touch with contemporary laws, which—rightly—are in place to guard the well-being of children today. However, in my view, it is impossible to face the full responsibilities of parenting and of blessing our children without at least making a basic acknowledgment of the need to bless by correcting.

The misunderstanding essentially revolves around the word derived from the old English translation of the Hebrew *shaybet,* which is used in the Old Testament in multiple ways—from the word for a king's scepter to describing everything from a branch of a family tree to a common stick. Translated "rod" in many Bible versions, the clear meaning of the biblical setting is far removed from seeing a rod as an instrument of brutality. The clearest meaning focuses the rod as a scepter, depicting the governmental role of a parent who will, as would a benevolent king, exercise all needed authority to protect his people. There is also a picture of a shepherd's staff in one Old Testament translation of "shaybet," which depicts guardian care and faithful, protective oversight.

That the Bible uses the word "rod" ("shaybet") in reference to the possible need for punishing a child is undeniable. But with equal honesty, the mood of the whole of the Scriptures, joined to the historic value for life within the Judeo-Christian tradition, makes it clear that the objective is not injury or even pain for pain's sake. Rather, the word "rod" exclusively appears in poetic passages of the Bible (the book of Proverbs) and contextually references the governmental and guardian role of the parent.

So it is that the issue of disciplining and correcting children, because it has been so often mishandled and so associated with brutal treatment, fails to be discussed or even considered by parents today. Unfortunately, this tends toward an equal and opposite error: breeding irresponsibility or passivity toward wise, gentle, yet forthright child discipline so that another form of child abuse occurs—neglected correction. The inevitable result is that many children never learn to respect authority or other people's property, rights or interests.

This plays well in those parts of today's culture dominated by philosophical relativism, where permissiveness and non- (or anti-) authoritarian attitudes dominate to the point of arguing that any other viewpoint suggests intolerance. Notwithstanding the fact that many social scientists are coming to acknowledge that so many of our current problems with youth run amuck are the result of these attitudes, God's ways are still regarded as suspect; and untutored parents are left without guidelines for applying godly discipline or, when necessary, punishment. These attitudes compromise patterns of godly thinking and living. As appropriately conceived laws intended for child protection proliferate, one is hard-pressed as a teacher of God's Word to know how to emphasize the importance of submitting to God's ways of disciplining children without being thought insensitive, sadistic or Neanderthal-like.

Still, to thoroughly deal with the subject of blessing your children, I felt it important to include a chapter for parents, one that specifically teaches the fact that it is impossible to bless your children without accepting the demands of disciplining them at times. Training and correcting children includes the practice of biblical discipline and a firm hand (the "rod," as earlier discussed) united to and exercised with love and affection. The result will beget a solidifying sense of security in a child—a goal worthy of taking time to weigh and find means to apply. These are the biblical guidelines that God Himself models and calls us to learn. The Word of God reveals that this is an integral part of His love and care for His children. He wants us to learn to do the same with our own children—He wants us to learn His magnificent balance of love and authority.

There is a difference between what the Bible calls being "raised" and simply "growing up." Every day a child's experiences are shaping something of the adult they will become, framing their attitudes, shaping their personalities. How we are raised—what values are made meaningful, what expectations are taught and shown to be livable and profitable—will exceed the effects of a child's heredity and environment if the child is raised in a relational atmosphere of spiritual substance joined to genuine human warmth and realism.

By examining this issue of godly authority, discipline and correction, I am seeking to provoke two strands of thought within the reader. First, I want to help parents make the necessary adjustments in their thinking to effectively apply the principles God has given us. Second, I want us to examine our hearts and see if there are areas where God wants to correct us, but we have been resisting Him. With His help, those aspects of our character that need shaping because of a past deficiency in the area of our own discipline can be corrected. With our obedience will come increased spiritual authority to learn how, as a parent, to cultivate obedience in our kids.

Benefiting from Correction

The word that is often used in the Bible to describe what we commonly call discipline is "chastening." It's a word that sounds somewhat archaic today—a word that tends to create vivid mental pictures in our minds that usually involve only physical punishment. But the concept of chastening in the Scriptures is never to damage or injure. According to Hebrews 12:11, it is to bring about "peaceable fruit"—which is a productive, fulfilling result. The purpose of chastening, although it evidences the authority of the party administering the correction, is not intended as a mere demonstration of strength. It is not to show who's boss. Neither is chastening intended to shatter a person's sense of value or demean their sense of self-esteem. It is a means of confronting persistent willfulness, stubbornness, rebellion or refusal to appropriately respect or acknowledge authority.

Chastening is a means by which parents may prevent their children from having to discover in far more painful ways that certain things in life carry severe penalties if ignored or abused. That facet of raising a child which involves an occasional need for chastening—though, remember, punishment is but a small part of child discipline—is to confront the child's unwillingness to come to terms with the realities of how life works.

Disciplining Your Child as an Act of Faith

Both Anna and I are second-generation Christians blessed with the advantage of having been raised in the ways of the Lord—a benefit that too few people enjoy. Having had that experience with our parents and having found such "raising" to be a blessing, we made the choice to raise our own kids that way too. It was, and is, a walk of faith. Seeing the fruit of righteousness develop in your children as they grow is a thrilling thing—and well worth the investment.

Bringing up children to observe the ways of the Lord is about more than just telling them they need to get saved. It means teaching them principles of love and authority, obedience and discipline. It is a relational priority that every parent must face up to, and it takes faith. Some parents are afraid of being strong with their children—of confronting, correcting or occasionally chastening—because they understandably do not want to hurt their kids. It's not easy to take the time and the thoughtfulness required to train a child in the Lord's ways. Even when it's necessary, it isn't easy to discipline a child.

I am very happy and humbled before God to see His Word fulfilled in our own four kids, all of whom are walking in His ways. None of our children went through any teenage rebellion or gave us any serious difficulty. We have never had to fight to get them to go to church. It wasn't because of some strict authoritarian regime that we imposed on them but because they were taught to think and make wise value judgments about how to live life to the fullest within a secure, godly framework.

Overcoming the Fear of Disciplining

In order to have godly authority as a parent, we first need to submit ourselves to the authority of God our Father. As we learn to accept His loving correction ourselves, we will administer it to our children all the more effectively. Unfortunately, the loving, disciplining work of God's hand in our lives is feared by some, either because of the absence of loving discipline ministered by earthly parents or because of abuse of such practices by a father figure. Yet, we need not fear our heavenly Father, whose Word promises that He has only our best interests at heart. The sooner we recognize in ourselves the things that are causing God grief and leading Him to chasten us (and we then respond to Him obediently), the sooner it will be over and the less severe it will be.

Chastening is the Lord's method of rescuing us from our foolishness; it is not His way of exerting His almightiness upon our vulnerability. God does not need to do that. Neither should we as parents abuse discipline by exercising authority for authority's sake, just to impose our will in a matter and squash our kids' ability to think for themselves.

Chastening God's Way

In the following section I have sought to outline five ways in which God chastens us. Seeing each in its biblical setting, as well as noting the sequence of procession in my outline, parents may be helped to serve the stewardship of their children's care and nurturing through applied good-sense discipline. If lovingly administered, we may well expect the fruit of "peaceableness" in our children and, even more, see this wisdom of the heavenly Father passed on to the next generation.

These five steps are in an ascending order of severity, intended—if wisely applied—to necessitate the next step if the preceding one is ineffective. Our experience, with that of a host of parents I know who have applied these principles, actually results in very rare occasions of the fifth step becoming necessary.

1. He Begins by Administering a Direct Instruction

Trust in the LORD with all your heart, and lean not on your own understanding; in all your ways acknowledge Him, and He shall direct your paths.

PROVERBS 3:5-6

God always begins by making plain His will and way for us by giving us direct instructions. He begins by speaking to our hearts through the Holy Spirit, who reveals the Father's will. All Christians can testify to the fact that, at one time or another, they have been aware of the force of truth in a passage or message from God's Word, charging them to do something—or to stop doing something.

All children will respond to the exertion of godly, parental influence.

The Father gives such direct instruction as we read our Bibles or as someone else teaches us from the Word and speaks with authority to our hearts. This is the first way He disciplines—teaching us as disciples who learn obedience by direct instruction.

My own father had a rule that he would never tell us children anything twice if he was correcting us. He always got our complete attention and only had to tell us something once. This is a valuable lesson for parents to learn. If you want children to stop doing something, first get their attention. It doesn't matter whether they're toddlers or teenagers, get their attention—make eye contact. Talk to their souls, not just their ears! You have to make children understand why you don't want them to do what they are doing. You can tell when they genuinely understand. And when they do, you need to hold them accountable to that understanding.

God speaks to us in the same way. You know when God has spoken to you and said, "This is My will." All children will respond to the exertion of godly, parental influence. Don't fear that they will hate you because you shape, correct or discipline them. God has put in each person a capacity to understand and relate to trusted authority. A child related to in this way will gain confidence and security and will not be moved to anger or hatred.

2. He Corrects Us by a Word or an Impression

Your ears shall hear a word behind you, saying,
"This is the way, walk in it," whenever you turn to the right
hand or whenever you turn to the left.

Isaiah 30:21

By the ministry of the Holy Spirit, God also corrects us by using a word or an impression. Accompanying His direct instruction to us concerning His will, He tends our souls with shaping instruction, which He uses to guide us or get us back on track.

It's incidental but interesting that I can snap my fingers quite loudly. This skill was a useful attention getter when our kids were growing up. Whenever I observed them doing something unacceptable, that snapping sound had an awesome warning power. Whether we were at home or out visiting, whenever our kids began to misbehave, that sound brought about an instant change in their actions. Whenever that snap occurred, the child would immediately look at me, knowing there was some directive or caution to be given. It wasn't always corrective; it was often simply an assist to maintain order or to signal the need for attentiveness to a matter. The Lord deals with us that way too: He does not let things go by lightly.

We always made a point of clearly explaining and guiding our children from a base of understanding, not merely doling out correction.

He corrects—and He is not bland in making these corrections. They will often come either by a word or an impression and—snap!—we recognize His prompting.

But life in our house wasn't simply a succession of finger snapping. Anna and I taught, discussed things with and guided our children. Our kids could tell by our reactions whether we approved of something or not; but we always made a point of clearly explaining and guiding them from a base of understanding, not merely doling out correction.

God wants us to use words or impressions in training our kids because none of us when we are taught, understand how to apply the lesson 100 percent without further correction and adjustment. Knowing the instructions is one thing; applying and living them out is another.

Some people think of correction as an insult. It's amazing how intimidated people can get when they are corrected. "I already knew that" is a favorite expression used by children. An adult will react in just the same way, only their response will be slightly more sophisticated. They may say, "Yeah, of course," or feign all kinds of things—irritation, anger, even deafness. Pride will always find ways to throw up barricades to correction, expressing itself in defensiveness or even hostility. But Jesus' instruction to you and me is to humble ourselves; and when we reach the place where we can admit that we can't do whatever it is on our own, then we ask for help and God graciously gives guidance and assistance. This model is worth adopting in training and developing our own children.

3. He Changes the Time We Can Go Somewhere or Do Something

Then the LORD said to Moses: "How long will these people reject Me? And how long will they not believe Me, with all the signs which I have performed among them?"

NUMBERS 14:11

The children of Israel were prevented from entering the Promised Land as a result of the Lord's chastening. He was forced to restrict them because of their disobedience. Sadly this process took 40 years to complete. In the same way, after both direct instruction and guiding instruction have taken place, we must follow the Lord's example and move on to restricting our children's freedom. Sometimes you have to say to your kids, "I'm sorry, but because of the way you've behaved, you're not going to be able to go to that party (or on that date or to the movies) with your friends."

This is an important and effective tool in training your children. Today many parents are drawn into the whirlwind of preoccupation that the average middle schooler or teenager has with his or her social life. In fact, the parents may have planted the seed themselves by forcing their toddlers into a busy schedule of classes, play dates and parties. Parents come to believe the lie that the whole world hinges on whether their children attend a particular event or not. Let me tell you—it doesn't! And by complying with your kids' requests to go to every event that pops up among their peers, you are robbing them of an important aspect of discipline and correction. Our kids need to learn that they can't just do as they please whenever they feel like it. Life does not work that way. Social events are important to our children, but what is more important is for them to learn and understand what really counts in life.

It is important when disciplining a child in this way that he or she knows and understands the reason for it and feels the loving correction of the parent. It must never be done with any sense of delight on the part of the parent but with concern for the child's well-being. Discipline administered in such a way will shape their lives for the good.

4. He Denies a Privilege and Withdraws It

> *Then the LORD spoke to Moses and Aaron,*
> *"Because you did not believe Me, to hallow Me in the eyes*
> *of the children of Israel, therefore you shall not bring this*
> *assembly into the land which I have given them."*
>
> NUMBERS 20:12

By denying a privilege, we are discussing more than the single method of issuing restrictions on a child's freedom to go somewhere or do something. A strategy that only says no doesn't necessarily make the desired point. Ask yourself what is needed to register full understanding. This measure of correction is not merely the deferment of some event until another time but is the complete withdrawal of a privilege and for sufficient time to register an appropriate degree of remorse, depending on the serious-ness of the issue.

Moses was disciplined by the Lord and didn't get to enter the Promised Land. It was the punishment for an impulsive flash of temper, a single presumptuous act. God can be tough! Does Moses' punishment seem harsh? Maybe it does, at least in our eyes. But the Lord had a good reason for it. In similar fashion, there may be times when your child thinks your punishment is too demanding. But take your position seriously. You know better—that's why you're the one doing the parenting. So don't step down to "kidding" with your correction.

With the passage of time, God expects us to learn and grow. The severity of His dealings with us over certain issues, therefore, becomes steeper. Over time, we ought to know and we ought to obey. God didn't discredit all that Moses had achieved in the past. In effect He was saying, "Moses, you've walked with Me long enough to know better than that." Denying a privilege altogether is a step further in the corrective process; it can be harsher and more painful.

This doesn't mean that we need to be scared of God, thinking that He will slam the door on all great opportuni-ties in our lives because of the slightest disobedience on our part. God deals with us like children, recognizing where we are and how we need to be dealt with, like the loving Father

He is. This is how we need to be with our kids too. No loving parent will wield the threat of loss of privileges to enforce their own will in a mean or cruel way. Nevertheless, a loving and corrective use of this sort of child discipline will sometimes call for drastic action that feels as hard for us to apply as it is for the child to receive. When that's the case, we need to be prepared to go through with the correction—all the way—for the child's ultimate benefit.

5. He Allows Physical Punishment by Lifting His Hand

> *The rod and rebuke give wisdom.*
> PROVERBS 29:15

It is important to realize that the chastening of God does not begin with physical punishment. That comes last, after every nonphysical method has been exhausted. This is the pattern God wants us to follow with our kids.

How does God punish us physically? He lifts His hand but not in the same way we might do it with our children. God's ways are always different from ours in that respect. Our ways imitate and shadow His ways imperfectly. God has His hand on your life already; and if it comes to the point where other forms of discipline have failed, then God will *lift His hand of blessing from you.* When that happens, we naturally experience the undesirable option—we get what He has been protecting us from. We become subject to affliction. By that term, I refer to all that would expose us to other than God's purpose and blessing: the diminishing of well-being, fruitfulness, happiness—the diminishing of God's covenanted "best" for our lives. When God's divine possibilities for our lives become unprotected from those things that bring about distress, pain, loss or even calamity, it isn't because He has reared back and slapped us down in an act of heavenly retribution. It's because we have proceeded beyond known boundaries to the point where He simply backs away, lifts His hand from us and says, "Then have your own way—and its consequences."

Please understand that I am not saying that every time a person gets sick or suffers a loss it's because he or she must have sinned. In John 9:1-3, Jesus made clear that this is not the case. Some sickness is just a natural part of life on a broken planet and is not to be regarded as necessarily having any spiritual implications. But many afflictions—including physical sickness—do occur as a result of God's lifting His hand in chastening. At other times, our finances may suffer for having violated the wisdom of His ways. Both of these—our bodies and our monies—are very effective ways for God to get our attention by lifting His hand of blessing. It is His effective rod of chastening.

The parental discipline of physical punishment administered in a loving, godly way should always take place within the context of caring communication with a child—assuring clear awareness of right and wrong on the issue. Taking the time to communicate this removes punishment from impulsive or temper-related action, thus assuring that the child grasps its depth of meaning and its judicious application. This will assure that the child is never injured or even bruised—either physically or emotionally. It avoids confusion and hurt feelings which, given place, can take root and warp other aspects of the parent-child relationship. So the "lifting" of a parent's hand is only to be used when all else has failed, and it is never administered in a fit of temper.

My counsel is cautious on this matter, not only because of the ease of being misunderstood, but because I am so convinced that this order of chastening need very rarely be applied. In reviewing Anna's and my years of raising our kids, such undesired but needed occasions were always measured moments—not impulsive outbursts. They rarely occurred and never were demeaning or injurious to our children. Our children's social and emotional stability, as well as their own parental success, are the best testimony to this—not to mention the beauty of our ongoing, uninterrupted depth of relationship with them to this day.

Caring for Gifts from the Lord

The Bible says that children are gifts from the Lord. No one takes a beautiful gift and demolishes it. We are given stewardship of a living, breathing, growing gift from God that comes to us with both an ability to receive the things of the Lord and the human liability of having been born with the fallen-sin nature of man. Godly shaping, training and discipline administered in an atmosphere of love and freedom deals realistically with the latter and assists the child in the former. Faithful, biblical, grace-filled instruction, joined to appropriately administrated discipline when necessary, is certain to make this combination a gift that keeps on giving to others long after the child becomes an adult.

It's an inheritance worth preserving and passing on to our children.

Prayer

Father God, I thank You for the children You have placed in my life and the trust in which You hold me to receive, steward and shepherd them. Help the windows of my soul to be clean of any of the world's dirt or grit so that Your light of wisdom can shine through me to them. Order my thoughts, my emotions, my lips and the works of my hands that they may reflect Your desire to see my children grow up knowing, living and loving Your way. Help me to overcome my resistance to administering godly correction and discipline by healing me of any past wounds so that I may walk in confidence to bless my children by following Your way. In Jesus' name, I pray. Amen.

CREATE AN ATMOSPHERE OF FREEDOM IN YOUR HOME

I am the LORD your God, who brought you out of the land of Egypt, out of the house of bondage.

EXODUS 20:2

We can hardly begin to imagine the elation of the children of Israel as they turned their backs on 400 years of slavery and hardship under the Egyptians and began their exodus. In the classic Cecil B. DeMille film *The Ten Commandments,* this event is vividly depicted when thousands of Israelites, rejoicing as they ride carts or donkeys or walk with their belongings piled on their backs, head for a life of freedom and hope. Still, harsh oppression and unreasonable rule upon generations of the children of Israel had vanquished any cohesive social or spiritual inheritance, and these people of Moses' day were tragically lacking an adequate understanding of how to live godly lives—or live successfully—in the "free" world. Though they were eager to live the new life ahead of them, they were neither spiritually nor emotionally prepared to proceed or to process its realities effectively. They were quite literally like children who need to be taught the very foundation principles, values and the way life works according to God's intended plan and purpose.

Establish Protective Boundaries

No child naturally knows how to live in a manner that brings blessing to themselves and others, but many parents today fail to recognize the need to teach this manner in a loving and systematic way to their kids. They falsely assume their kids will just pick it up as they go along. It's true that kids will pick things up as they go along; but unless a parent orders what those things are, kids will generally pick up things that will require their adult lifetime to overcome.

Then there are the parents who think they have to wait until the child is older before beginning spiritual, moral and social training. These parents miss the opportunity to instill in their kids the normal acceptance of values, principles and practices of Spirit-filled Christian living when they are at their most vulnerable and receptive age.

The Lord reminded the children of Israel that He delivered them from the house of bondage as a preface to giving them the Ten Commandments—the parameters designed specifically to help them learn how to establish normal family life in an orderly society. The Lord's intention in setting forth His Law was not to place oppressive restrictions but to set up protective boundaries against anything that would attempt to encroach upon

> *God's commandments are like the owner's manual for the proper living of life.*

the liberty into which He had delivered them. The Law was given to keep them from becoming ensnared in personal and spiritual bondage, even worse than Egypt's slavery. These boundaries would let the people become liberated by God's Law to live their lives to the fullest, as He intended for them.

God's commandments are like the owner's manual for the proper living of life. They provide a framework that enables God's children—and ours—to grow up sound minded, to establish healthy relationships, to demonstrate good character, to have a life of fulfillment and satisfaction and to establish a home of freedom instead of a home of bondage.

Enjoy Heaven in Your Home

In Deuteronomy, God outlined workable details so that the children of Israel could know how to obey the commandments He had established. He gave them rich promises for the blessings that would distill upon them and their children if they would teach them His laws.

> Therefore you shall lay up these words of mine in your heart and in your soul, and bind them as a sign on your hand, and they shall be as frontlets between your eyes. You shall teach them to your children, speaking of them when you sit in your house, when you walk by the way, when you lie down, and when you rise up. And you shall write

them on the doorposts of your house and on your gates, that your days and the days of your children may be multiplied in the land of which the LORD swore to your fathers to give them, like the days of the heavens above the earth (Deut. 11:18-21).

The same principles apply today. God says that if we will teach our children to respect, honor and live by His laws, then we can expect the following blessings for ourselves and for them:

- Both our lives and the lives of our children will be long.
- He has a land that has been promised to us.
- Our days on Earth will be like those of heaven.

God calls His children—you and me—to establish for our children something of heaven in the home, an atmosphere of freedom created by our parental commitment to the following two things:

- *To establish our homes* upon the principles that secure spiritual liberty. As with Israel, these same principles summed up in the Ten Commandments still provide practical life patterns that

bring true freedom, fruitfulness and fulfillment
into human experience.

- *To lead our children* to understand and live in
those principles so that in time they will order
their own homes in the same way, passing along
a spiritual inheritance from generation to generation.

It has been remarkable for Anna and me to watch
how, in our own family, our children and our grandchildren have learned and continue to live life God's way. It is
an incredible privilege to witness the succession and the
impact of God's inheritance of blessing—from Jack and
Dolores (my parents) and Elmer and Emma (Anna's parents) to the two of us and then to our four kids—Rebecca,
Jack, Mark and Christa. Now we witness that same inheritance of blessing in the lives of our 11 grandchildren. The
effect of godliness in a home can initiate a chain reaction
of heaven exploding into Earth!

Because home and family are always central in God's
plan to provide people with happiness, health, holiness
and hope, Scripture is the centerpiece that shows us His
concern for and the importance He places upon the family. It also provides His clarity of teaching in order to lead
us in living and relaying His ways.

Seek God's Way

In the Old Testament we see this concern for family exemplified in the relationship among Abraham, Isaac and Jacob. Throughout the Bible, the Lord refers to Himself as the God of Abraham, Isaac and Jacob, and by that He is making and highlighting a statement: He didn't just make a covenant with individuals but with a family. He is also underscoring the fact that Abraham blessed his son, Isaac, by successfully transmitting God's ways to him. Isaac did the same with his son Jacob. All three men had their own occasions of failure as parents (as do you and I), but still they conveyed with a degree of fidelity the ways of the Lord to the next generation. As demonstrated in the lives of these historic men of God, there is hope for us while we are seeking God's way.

Another example that closely parallels this principle is found in the New Testament and comes, as far as we know, from a single-parent family. If Timothy, the apostle Paul's protégé, had a father who was living, he was evidently not a man who was living for the Lord. Twice in the Scriptures there are references to Timothy's upbringing. In Paul's second letter to Timothy, he gave thanks for Timothy's "genuine faith . . . which dwelt first in your grandmother Lois and your mother Eunice"

(2 Tim. 1:5). Paul also mentioned in 2 Timothy 3:15 that Timothy knew the Scriptures "from childhood." Timothy was raised in the Lord's ways by his mother and grandmother, who were the spiritual influences in his life. It seems that his father was absent for some reason that we are not told; this provides hope for those who are not in a traditional family setting that it is still possible to raise children in the ways of the Lord and see them flourish and prosper.

Live Out the Ways of God

The challenge for all parents is to model a life of obedience to God in their family and to demonstrate the practical ways of the Lord to their children. One thing that has powerfully impacted the ongoing spiritual development of our family over the years has been the discipline of having Communion at home.

It is a good thing to raise your kids with a familiarity of the sacrament of the Lord's Table. In our own home as I was growing up, taking Communion was not done according to any particular pattern but was initiated by my parents when we were facing a hard time as a family, or to celebrate and thank the Lord for something special. This discipline was naturally carried over into the raising of our own kids. We did it whenever we were facing a spiritual struggle and needed to hear from God.

I realized the power of sharing the Lord's Table as a family many years ago when I first began to pastor The Church On The Way in 1969. We had arrived at the church and were preparing to move into the parsonage. As we inspected it for the first time, we noticed there was one door in the hallway that was newer than all the rest—the one opening into the bathroom. The broker showing us the home explained that the son of the previous occupants had returned from Vietnam suffering severe mental and emotional trauma and had become a habitual user of marijuana. He would often lock himself in the bathroom where he would smoke. His parents couldn't stop him.

One day, in this depleted mental state, intoxicated and certainly out of his right mind, he became so frantic and driven by fear that he locked himself in the bathroom and collapsed there. It required emergency personnel to tear down the door in order to rescue him. Hearing this, I at first saw this tragic story as merely the explanation of a markedly different door in the hallway, perceiving nothing in particular to do about it. But something soon happened that changed that.

About six weeks after we moved into the house, it seemed that sickness would never go away. Our entire family went through a frustrating cycle of illness—one member after another succumbed to one malady or another. Finally, after the fourth of the six of us became sick, I woke up one morning, alerted by an insight I knew the Lord had given me. I realized that God was instructing me with wisdom, showing me that a spirit of affliction was in our house and needed to be dealt with—and revealing to me that this was related to the activities of the previous occupants' son. Of course, physical sickness can come from anywhere and at any time and can simply occur for very natural reasons. But it is biblically true, and wise to understand and be aware, that the adversary's tactics also advance where evil spirits administrate terrain given to them. In such a situation, God has shown us how to reclaim the turf and see His kingdom established and to witness the supplanting of the work of the enemy.

Looking back on this, it surprised me when I discovered a point of neglect—not consistent with what would have been our usual practice. As a family we had not yet had Communion together in our new home! It was obviously time to do so, and I knew that by that means we would not only be blessed in our worship but would also be taking spiritual action that would cleanse any evil residue from our dwelling.

I want to emphasize that I did not prepare a family Communion service because I'm a pastor but because we all were Christians. We began our worship by sharing the Lord's Table in that tiny little bathroom, explaining to our kids what we were doing and why we were doing it. We did not make it scary nor relate the matter superstitiously. But it is important to explain to children the why and the how of dealing with spiritual issues, to help them grow in their understanding as well as their behavior. We told our children that, in the past, bad things had happened in that room and that the Lord had alerted us to pray and to praise Jesus, claiming the power of His blood to cleanse it. We didn't say to our kids, "There are demons in that room!" It is never worthy to focus on the adversary or his cohorts. Always focus on Jesus, and thus avoid fear and release with spiritual confidence and power.

We simply explained the dynamics of spiritual victory and the power of the Cross, not only to save and forgive us, but also to keep and deliver us from evil.

So it was that we simply explained, on a level our children could understand, the dynamics of spiritual victory and the power of the Cross, not only to save and forgive us, but also to keep and deliver us from evil. And incidentally, immediately after we took Communion together, the family member who was sick at that time was healed and the cycle of recurring illness in the family ceased.

The point of this example is that parents need to live out spiritual realities like this in a manner that becomes an ordinary and natural part of family life so that the kids can learn from and imitate it. Other ways to bless your children in this regard include teaching them to tithe their allowance and encouraging them in Bible reading and devotions, not only with the entire family, but also on their own. This helps each child learn to develop his or her own personal relationship with the Lord. Living out the ways of God must be tightly woven into the fabric of family life.

Avoid the Obstacles That Hinder Spiritual Freedom

There are two major obstacles that we as parents need to confront in order to enjoy an atmosphere of freedom in our homes. The first is concerned with ensuring that, in our personal lives, we are free from the influence of sin; the second has to do with protecting the boundaries of our homes from ungodly influences.

Failure or Pollution of Our Own Family Line

This is a reality established with clarity in the Scriptures. Much of the sin and pollution that takes place in families is transmitted *generationally*. Many believers have not received instruction in regard to this subject. Generational sin, while not a concept intended to suggest that what is transmitted through families provides an excuse for sin or removes an individual's responsibility for his or her own sin, is still important to spiritual understanding. It essentially relates to what God warned us about when He said in Exodus 20:5 and Deuteronomy 5:9 that He is a jealous God who visits judgment for the sins "of the fathers upon the children to the third and fourth generations."

A superficial view of the text suggests that God is speaking of a vindictive attitude He will carry into the future for sins committed by individuals. That isn't His point at all. In effect, He is saying, "I am giving you these laws, not only to make your life profitable, but also to remove the impact of your failure on future generations." He is instructing in the reality of a "spiritual genetic," as it were, basically advising that as certainly as hair and eye color and other physical features are generationally transmitted, so are the effects of sin and the tendency to repeat certain sins within a family line.

So sin has a trickle-down effect—one that will contaminate successive generations unless it is dealt with by the blood of Jesus. However, I want each reader to rise with me in praise to the Savior for what He has done through His complete triumph on the cross. Joined to repentance for our part in any survival of a particular family trait of recurring sin pattern, we—and our offspring—can be cleansed, delivered and released into a future without this baggage of sin's impact on our family line.

If you believe that you may be suffering the consequences of generational sin, get together with a trusted friend or church leader to talk and pray it through. Claim the liberating power of the cross of Jesus Christ in your life and lay hold of the freedom that Jesus has already won for you. Pray over your children as well and ask the Lord to loose them from any ungodly generational influences.

Ungodly Things Tolerated in the Home

In the homes of even reasonably dedicated Christians there can be a lapse in moral and spiritual standards. The parents may watch unsuitable TV programs or videos and the kids wind up seeing them too. This is harmful to both children and parents. The output of television is one of the most polluting influences in children's lives today. We have lost our sense of offense at blasphemy, profanity and immorality;

we have lost our sense of outrage at the world's casual attitude toward human sexuality. Sometimes we gloss over the use of foul language in a movie because we just want to watch it. We make the excuse, "Well, they've only said that a few times." But how many times would you tolerate a member of your family saying it in your house? The fact is, it is being said in your house and your kids are learning from it. Just because it's coming off a DVD or a videotape doesn't lessen its impact.

The key is for parents to watch TV programs and videos with their kids, helping them to understand God's way in contrast to what they have just seen or heard.

I am sympathetic to the fact that it is very difficult to see anything enjoyable on television without running into some kind of sexual innuendo or other offensive content. But that kind of influence runs contrary to an atmosphere of spiritual life in the home. Should we then just unplug our sets? Maybe it will soon come to that. In the meantime, what should a parent do?

I believe the key is for parents to watch TV programs and videos with their kids and talk about them, helping the kids to understand God's way in contrast to what they have just seen or heard.

We have watched many TV programs and films with our children and run into a moment when there was something we wished had not been said. When that occurred, we would stop what we were watching and use those times as teaching moments. If it was a video, we would pause the tape and say, "Let Dad and Mom explain something to you here." We wouldn't prevent our children from continuing to watch the movie, but we would educate them that what we had just seen or heard was not how we acted or thought as people of God. We would also get feedback from the kids to see if they had grasped the issue and understood the godly attitude toward what they had just seen or heard. These distinctions can only be made by a parent who takes the time to correct and guide a child.

Be like the Watchman

In Luke 12:39, Jesus, speaking about His return, uses the analogy of the master of a house being watchful so that the house will not be broken into. In the same way, we need to guard and protect the spiritual boundaries of our home to ensure they are preserved and that nothing encroaches on our home that doesn't belong there.

Parents who know and believe the ways of the Lord are the best equipped to bless their children. Children will inherit from us either a passion for the things of God or a casual attitude toward spirituality. For a household to thrive in an atmosphere of freedom, parents must be living examples of godly discipline and impart the richness and profitability of those values to their children. Let your heart be gripped with a desire for vital, Spirit-filled life in your home. Then your children will grow up to become liberated adults who are secure in themselves because they know and understand what makes life work.

Prayer

Dear Lord God, I am filled with gratitude for the provision of Your Law, the grace accomplished by Your Son and the equipping work of Your Holy Spirit in my life. Thank You for showing me how to teach my children to be free from the hopeless pursuits of the world and the bondage they bring. Deepen my sensitivity to the needs of my children and give me discernment about any ungodly influences that may be lingering in my home. Bless our family to walk in one accord on these matters, and strengthen our love and respect for one another every day. In Jesus' name, I pray. Amen.

Chapter Seven

SPEAKING BLESSINGS ON YOUR CHILDREN

It is perhaps among the most humbling features of God's ways with humankind that He confers upon us a staggering degree of power (and responsibility) in the capacity of our words to cause things to happen. It is within the broad scope of this remarkable truth that the privilege and the power of speaking blessings upon our children come into view.

From the opening words of the Bible, the power of the spoken word is in evidence. In essence, words are not only the means *by* which creation is made, but they are also the substance—the stuff—*of* which the tangible realm is shaped. "And God said" appears in the Genesis text, and the next thing, *what* God said appears in our world.

The power of words is not only evident when God uses them in creating, but it is also evident in His ways that teach us how to live in that creation. All of the Father's laws are essentially God's guidelines to make life "work" in the realm He has created for man's fruitfulness and fulfillment.

- When obedience aligns with those laws, the power of God's divine order *advances* the beauty of His intended blessing and the force of His words (laws) function *for* us—effectively releasing the divine intention for ever-expanding dimensions of human enrichment and joy.

- In contrast, when disobedience refuses God's laws, the opposite of blessing ensues. The "curse"— i.e., the penalty of disobedience—is not so much a direct action of God's punishment as it is the raw impact felt when sin invokes the *reversal* of God's order; it is as if the power of His words runs backward *against* the divine design and shrinks the boundaries of God's intended blessing.

Thus, the power of words is seen in both our creation as beings, planned by our creator, and our instruction as children, beloved by our Father. And it is in this light that the power of our words can best be understood.

A Choice to Speak "Life"!

Proverbs 18:21 teaches us, "Death and life are in the power of the tongue, and those who love it will eat its fruit." The profundity of this truth is seen in all of life. Kind words breed warmth of relationship; harsh words breed tension and separation. True words build trust and confidence; lies break trust and doubt, and suspicion replaces confidence. In fact, words are central to our most meaningful relationships:

- We confidently and readily do business with people whom we can affirm are ones who keep their word. People who don't do this dissolve the grounds for their own enduring success.
- We build friendships with those who understand our *hearts* as well as our lips—who truly perceive what we mean when we say the words we say and relate to us by fully grasping the spirit of our spoken words.

- We establish our marriage covenants with an oath, which according to God's Word is to be an abiding commitment of truthfulness and fidelity and which, if broken, brings a frightening breakdown of the oath's power.
- We teach our children what is right, and with those words we seek to relay the very principles of God's order so that His blessing will be *advanced* and not *reversed* as they grow from year to year.

In all these regards, *life* is transmitted, experienced and multiplied when the tongue speaks its truth and love, while *death* is inevitable otherwise—through shrinking, withering, suffocating or killing what should or might have been.

The Power of Speaking Blessing

Early in the Bible, the power of God's people to speak blessing upon one another is clearly shown. Noah blesses Shem and Japheth for their respect, rather than mockery, of his dignity as their father (see Gen. 9:26-27). Melchizedek blesses Abraham for honoring God for His protection and victory and for Abraham's tithing instead of conceding to the offers of the king of Sodom to take the goods for himself (see Gen. 14:18-24). Repeatedly, God tells Abraham that his offspring will be instruments of blessing to the whole world—both in their deeds as well as with their words (see Gen. 12:3; 18:18; 22:16-18).

From these early experiences, the understanding of the power of blessing began to develop and we see it becoming a practice of parents toward their children. Isaac evidences the depth and meaning of this practice in his attentiveness to purposefully minister such a blessing to his sons (see Gen. 27). Notwithstanding the twists the story takes, the underlying fact is that this practice of blessing was seen as not only something God would hear and enforce, but it also was something very determinative in the child's life.

The principle is clear: God has given parents the privilege and the power to speak blessing upon their children and, with that blessing, to advance life, health, growth, joy and self-confidence! We need to learn to steward this privilege as a dynamic aspect of raising our children and blessing them in every way that we can.

Ways to Bless Your Children

The first order of blessing is reflected by the simplest things we might do, which, though seemingly ordinary, carry an immense weight in telling children they are loved, cared for, valued and being "looked over" (rather than over-looked).

Remember those childhood experiences when you simply sensed the approval or care of a parent or loved one? We can learn from the ultimate Father by noting how He blesses us with His attentions in distinct ways that parallel our warmest memories as children when someone blessed us in simple yet affirming ways:

- An arm over the shoulder, or an embrace in a time of disappointment or fear (see Deut. 33:27)
- A pat on the back or a firm steadying hand at a crucial moment (see Ps. 139:5)
- A whisper in the ear, giving quiet assurance or secret instructions (see Isa. 30:21)
- A snug tucking in bed when surrounded by the darkness of night (see Ps. 127:2-3)
- A kiss on the cheek, or being dandled on a parent's knee (see Ps. 103:13—"pities" is translated from the Hebrew word *rawcham,* which means to tenderly love or caress)

However, the most affirming are those blessings that come in *words*: (1) words that affirm and approve, (2) words that commend and compliment, (3) words that specifically speak love and affection, (4) words that invoke hope and self-confidence, and (5) words that answer pain and disappointment with support and faith.

Learn the Bible Basics

The fountainhead blessing in the Bible is found in Numbers 6:24-26. This is the blessing God ordained that the priests of Israel would use to speak blessing in His name over His own children, whom He called the children of Israel.

First, I call this the fountainhead blessing because this blessing was transmitted to every succeeding generation for use and exercise by faith, right down to the present moment as we speak it with privileged boldness. The New Testament clearly reveals that *every* believer in Christ not only is *now* called holy—a saint in Christ (see Rom. 1:7; 1 Cor. 1:2)—but also is *now* bestowed the office of a priest (A minister *to* God in worship and *for* God to others (see 1 Pet. 2:5,9; Rev. 1:5-6). This is the Bible's authoritative grounds for us to speak blessing, knowing that the power of God's eternal word and promise are backing up that blessing—that our Father stands fully ready to enforce and apply all its implications unto the full dimensions of their blessed intention.

Second, this blessing is a fountainhead because the ideas contained in it overflow with so much meaning that, if it is understood and not merely repeated, it becomes a warm and powerful invocation loaded with promise and power. Repeat Numbers 6:24-26 with me, and then examine its depth:

> The LORD bless you and keep you; the LORD make His face shine upon you, and be gracious to you; the LORD lift up His countenance upon you, and give you peace.

The rich dimension of this blessing deserves the understanding and the conscious desire to commend its scope of goodness upon those over whom it is spoken. Consider the individual phrases:

> **The LORD bless you and keep you:** The thrice-referenced *Lord* in whose name this blessing is offered is the God of the universe; He is *unlimited* in His capacity to prosper the efforts of those He *blesses*, and He is *unrestricted* in His power to protect those He *keeps*. (It is perfectly appropriate to add the name of your child after "you": e.g., "The Lord bless you and keep you, Mary.")

The LORD make His face shine upon you: His face, which shines "like the sun shining in its strength" (Rev. 1:16), radiates with His glory—a glory that goes before us, defends from behind us and overspreads us with the excellence of His presence (see Isa. 4:5; 58:8).

And be gracious to you: These words commend the one so blessed to receive the unmeasured bounty of God's *grace,* which is that quality of God's nature that not only bespeaks His will to show a forgiveness we do not deserve (see Eph. 2:8), but also that readiness to confer upon us the qualifying capability to receive daily power for living that we do not possess. This power sustains us "until the day of Jesus Christ" (Phil. 1:6-7).

The LORD lift up His countenance upon you: Again, the Lord—the One and only maker of heaven and Earth, our Savior Redeemer and the King of the universe—is now invited to allow His smile of approval to surround the individual being blessed. His countenance shines with love upon His own and when directed against evil, scatters the power of the enemy's efforts to curse (see Prov. 16:15; 20:8).

And give you peace: God's peace is a guardian that preserves the soul in the same way a sentry stands watch at his post (see Phil. 4:6-7). Further, His peace describes that progressive infusion of His multidimensional wholeness of spirit, soul and body, thus affording that every aspect of an individual's being or personality may live within the security of God's peaceable kingdom (see Isa. 32:18).

Speak These Blessings *Often!*

Have regular times when you lay your hands upon your child's head, gently (even quietly, while they sleep). Speak (or even whisper) the words with the quiet confidence that (1) you are privileged by the living God to declare this blessing, and (2) God Himself will attend to the word spoken because it is *His* Word you are speaking according to His will.

Avoid letting this practice become either a legalistic exercise (as though to remember after a time that it would have been appropriate to declare the blessing, but you did not, and thereby you have opened your child to a curse) or a ritualistic exercise (utilized so often that it becomes meaningless, if not annoying, by reason of a seeming redundancy of habit). The formation of a habit of blessing is not unworthy, but variety in conferring the blessing may be very desirable.

To assist in achieving variety, consider varying your blessing by invoking different compound names of the Lord and praying for Him to apply the power evident in each term to the need of the child. Listed below are the most commonly referenced compound names of Jehovah, the trait of His person to which each refers and a suggestion of how to use the name:

Jehovah-Jireh—The Lord Our Provider (see Gen. 22:14): Speak a blessing in the face of specific need, whatever realm the need may represent.

Jehovah-Raah—The Lord Our Shepherd (see Ps. 23:1): Speak a blessing with the reminder of God's never-forsaking presence and protection.

Jehovah-Shalom—The Lord Our Peace (see Judg. 6:24): Speak a blessing that will comfort in the midst of turmoil or upset.

Jehovah-Rapha—The Lord Our Healer (see Exod. 15:26): Speak a blessing that calls for God's grace of healing, knowing that He *wants* to heal the sick.

Jehovah-Nissi—The Lord Our Victory (see Exod. 17:15): Speak a blessing that reminds the child that the battle is not theirs but the Lord's.

Jehovah-Tsidkenu—The Lord Our Righteousness (see Ps. 23:3): Speak a blessing that declares how justice (righteousness) will come from God, even when unfair circumstances seem to be dominating.

Jehovah-Shammah—The Lord Is Present (see Ezek. 48:35): Speak a blessing which deepens the assurance of the Lord's attendant care and keeping presence.

As you bless, always see that your demeanor conveys the spirit and heart of our loving, living God. He not only wants to bless that child, but He also has called you and me to accept the responsibility for directly *inviting* that blessing.

The *expression* on your face, the *tone* with which you speak, the *touch* of your hand placed upon the child's head or shoulder, and the *time* and *timing* of your conferral of the blessing—all should be appropriate to the moment and contribute to the child's sense of being loved because they are being blessed.

Prayer

Father, I am astounded by the wonder of Your will and ways, that You would confer upon me the overwhelming privilege of being Your representative in both announcing and pronouncing Your blessing upon a child. As I receive this truth and am open to a willing exercise of its marvel-filled and powerful potential, I make this declaration: You are my God, and it is Your almighty throne I honor in this action of blessing children. I denounce any notion that my words are the source of the power in this blessing, but I also deny any idea that suggests my words are unimportant in this dramatic transaction. The fact that You make me your middleman, reaching to heaven—to Your throne and then to a child, who is Your created wonder and given to me to love and serve—is an awesome wonder in my sight. And so I ask You to help me minister blessings always with wisdom, always with faith and always with that gentle grace that will cause the children in my life to know by that blessing how beloved they are by You and by me.

In Your holy name. Amen.

Chapter Eight

DECLARE HIS
WONDROUS WORKS
TO YOUR CHILDREN

*O God, You have taught me from my youth; and to this day I
declare Your wondrous works. Now also when I am old and
grayheaded, O God, do not forsake me, until I declare Your
strength to this generation, Your power to everyone who is to come.*

PSALM 71:17-18

During one recent summer, Anna and I decided to make
the rounds and visit all of our children and their kids, by

virtue of our frequent flyer miles. We were excited as we anticipated the times we would share together—fun side trips and catching-up conversations, especially with our children who live far from us and whom we rarely see. As we planned the trip, it began to dawn on me that, as our family had become scattered geographically and were growing up much faster than seemed possible, there were Hayford "tribal" stories I wanted to be certain we relayed to them while Anna and I were still able.

Tribal Stories to Relate and Preserve

Tribal stories are the oral tradition passed down through the generations that relate the pivotal points of family history. By describing things that have happened through the years, these stories explain much about how the family has arrived at its own unique shape, values, understanding and ways.

I was feeling the deep desire to relay the stories, insights and impressions that I wanted to be sure our grandchildren would remember about us—stories that, by reason of the drama or interest in them, the kids would carry with them as their family legacy and feel strengthened by when they faced the joys and challenges in their own adult lives. The stories weren't intended to make them love Grandma and Grandpa more but to deepen their love and appreciation for Father God and the remarkable mercies and mighty works He has made manifest in our family—things that are so directly related to the very existence of each of those grandkids.

While musing on this, I looked into the Scriptures that counsel us about such "relaying," and my understanding was enlightened along lines I have never before seen so clearly.

When wisdom from the Bible can be paralleled with a parent's personal testimony, it registers biblical truth in a child in a way nothing else can.

The Bible encourages us to declare God's wondrous works, His strength and His power to the next generation; but I began to realize that it's not just talking about or telling them stories from the Bible. I believe we are instructed as well to give them a rich inheritance of our own testimonies of God's deliverance, victories and grace. Understanding Bible stories is an important part of a child's spiritual development and should never be minimized. But what Anna and I have realized over the years is that it's been the personal storytelling of what the Lord has done for us that really carried impact and weight with our kids.

When wisdom from the Bible can be paralleled with a parent's personal testimony—facing a trial or receiving a blessing—it registers biblical truth for a child in a way nothing else can. It's no longer just a story about what happened to somebody else a long time ago; it hits home. Making the application of God's Word immediate and relevant by telling your children the story of something that happened to you will help form the foundation of their spiritual inheritance. Telling your family's tribal stories to your kids makes the work of the Lord active and alive to them and helps them recognize that His blessings are present and available today.

When it's appropriate, don't be afraid to let your kids become part of the story as well. Then add it to the stories you remember together as a family. When you face a challenge your children can understand, include them in your prayer time about it. When you've received a victory or blessing, rejoice with them. Teach them to see that what we all go through in ordinary life is related to God's grace. Help them to develop stories of their own by encouraging them—as they are able—to share with the rest of the family how God, His Word and His Holy Spirit has helped them.

The Praises of the Lord

I will open my mouth in a parable; I will utter dark sayings of old, which we have heard and known, and our fathers have told us. We will not hide them from their children, telling to the generation to come the praises of the LORD, and His strength and His wonderful works that He has done.

PSALM 78:2-4

Psalm 78 begins with a commitment by the psalmist to tell "the generation to come the praises of the LORD." He then goes on to tell the stories of how God moved among His people from the time of Jacob all the way up until his own generation. He was sharing with his children the inheritance of all that had gone on before him—as his father had, no doubt, shared with him. Of course, all those stories referenced by the psalmist are stories of the family of Israel through the centuries, and there is no question that it is important that we know them and learn from them. But I believe the Holy Spirit, in giving us the directive to relay stories of God's great works, is not only giving a call to teach our children Bible stories, but He is also instructing us to tell them our family stories. It is glorifying to God and has a dramatic impact on your children when they hear and learn of the things that God did for Mom and Dad, for Grandma and Grandpa and for Great-Grandma and Great-Grandpa—stories about how God's hand has been on your family.

Six Kinds of Stories to Tell Our Children

The Bible reveals six kinds of stories to tell the children in our lives. Look at these with me, and then resolve in your heart to become a storyteller of the wonders God has performed on your behalf, and tell those things to the kids in your life.

1. Tell Your Children How the Lord Saved You

> And you shall observe this thing as an ordinance for you and your sons forever. . . . And it shall be, when your children say to you, "What do you mean by this service?" that you shall say, "It is the Passover sacrifice of the LORD, who passed over the houses of the children of Israel in Egypt when He struck the Egyptians and delivered our households" (Exod. 12:24-27).

The Lord instructed the children of Israel that their deliverance from the slavery and oppression of Egypt would be relived through what is today called the Passover Seder. He said to repeat the story from generation to generation so that there would be a systematic remembrance from year to year when the children asked, "Why do we do this? What does this mean?" The Seder was established as an opportunity for parents to tell their children, "We do it so that we never forget how the Lord delivered and saved us. It is how our family became a free people and how God showed His power to us."

This revelation in God's Word is sufficient to guide us to apply this wisdom. Clearly, we as believing adults should arrange ways and means to provide periodic occasions with our kids to tell our story. Our testimony will excite their curiosity and become registered in their minds for a lifetime.

I have marveled at the number of times children in a Communion service at our church will become intrigued by the presence of little cups of wine and want to ask, "What is this? Why are we doing it?" In our homes, as well, there should be special occasions in which all the family participates and the children have the event explained to them. It has always been bewildering to me that some church traditions oppose their people celebrating the Lord's Table in their own homes with their family (especially since that's the way it all began, both in the Old and

the New Testament). I do not believe such times are a substitute for worship with the congregation, but I do believe
they afford a distinct opportunity for children to hear
how their parents came to know the Lord and what are the
redemptive goals of their family.

This concept of telling your children takes me back to
childhood as I remember the many times our family
would ride together in the car—Daddy and Mamma in the
front and us kids in the back—and they would begin to
sing. One of the songs I most remember is one I learned as
I heard them singing,

> I am happy today, and the sun shines bright.
> The clouds have been rolled away;
> For the Savior said whosoever will
> May come with Him to stay.[1]

It's a heart-touching memory for me, because they would
tell us, "This is the song that was sung the night we received
Jesus as our Savior." They would each contribute to the testimony, but Mamma related that as she read the words
"whosoever will may come," she realized that "whosoever"
meant her.

They told us their story; and now, over 60 years after
the event they described, I'm telling it to you. The dynamic

of the testimony was that I not only was taught what salvation is by reading John 3:16, but I also was told by my parents, "This salvation happened to us!" Such telling your children of God's wondrous works fixes it in their minds. Watch for opportunities to tell your story to any children you influence. Tell them of the wonder of your salvation.

2. Tell Your Children About the Lord's Miraculous Provision for You

Then Moses said, "This is the thing which the LORD has commanded: 'Fill an omer with it, to be kept for your generations, that they may see the bread with which I fed you in the wilderness, when I brought you out of the land of Egypt.'"

EXODUS 16:32

Throughout their journey through the wilderness, the Lord miraculously provided the children of Israel with their daily bread called manna. Even more miraculous, God provided a double portion on the sixth day so that His children could rest in observance of the Sabbath. In Exodus 16:32, Moses tells Aaron that God has directed them to set aside a portion of manna that will be kept as a testimony to future generations of the goodness of His provision.

I remember a story my mother told me about how God provided for our family not long after she and my dad came to Christ. It was during the Great Depression of the 1930s. From week to week there was never any certainty about whether or not Daddy would have work. He and Mamma had just begun to tithe and were committed to obedience in that regard, even though they didn't know when Daddy's next paycheck was coming. The human inclination would have been to hold back this small portion for themselves, considering that finances were so unsteady and they had a baby to care for; but my parents believed the Word of the Lord and had chosen to walk in His ways.

I was taught the story of how the day came when there was no money and no food in the house. They prayed, "Lord, we just simply trust You, because You have promised You will provide for us." That young couple, fledglings in Christ, opened their door that morning and found a bag of groceries on the porch. They had no idea who had left the groceries. Though they had expressed their need to no one, somehow God had moved someone to bring the gift that answered their prayer. That story stimulated my faith until Anna and I had similar stories to tell our own children.

The story my parents told me is very simple, I realize, and I could easily tell you other stories of million-dollar miracles in our church. But there's no story that is more significant to me than the one about one bag of groceries on a front porch. Why? Because it relates how God began to move in a family—*my* family. It tells how a young couple in need stood faithful to trust God, even when the human argument would lead to taking another course. God continues to do the same wherever people trust. So tell your story—tell your children the stories of God's miraculous provision for you.

3. Tell Your Children How You've Failed but the Lord Forgave You

The censers of these men who sinned against their own souls, let them be made into hammered plates as a covering for the altar. Because they presented them before the LORD, therefore they are holy; and they shall be a sign to the children of Israel.

NUMBERS 16:38

In Numbers 16 we read a story about a group of men who decided to carry the censers containing the incense used in worshiping God in the way they wanted—not in the way God had commanded. The Bible says that instantly a devastating judgment fell on them. Following the judgment, the Lord commanded that the censers they had used be hammered out to make a cover for the brazen altar, the place of sacrifice where the sin offering was made. So it was done.

The Lord had the censers placed at the brazen altar as a double reminder: first, that any rebellion that proposes the attitude "I know better than God how to live" is eventually "flattened"—that is, hammered out; and second, as the story takes place where sacrifice for sin was offered, it points to the picture of how sinful rebellion can be forgiven and covered through the sacrifice of the blood. In the text of the story and in directing that the censers be fashioned into the covering for the altar, God explained why he commanded it: "They [the censers] shall be a sign to the children of Israel."

This presents us with another theme to carry through as we tell our children the stories of our lives. We are to tell of our failures, of our past and of how we rebelled against the Lord's way. We must tell how we were "flattened out" because of sin and how those sins were confessed and placed before Him and were covered by the blood of Jesus.

Tell stories that teach your children the folly of rebellion and of God's mercy and forgiveness.

4. Tell Your Children How God Has Guided You

Cross over before the ark of the LORD your God into the midst of the Jordan, and each one of you take up a stone on his shoulder, according to the number of the tribes of the children of Israel, that this may be a sign among you when your children ask in time to come, saying, "What do these stones mean to you?" Then you shall answer them that the waters of the Jordan were cut off before the ark of the covenant of the LORD; when it crossed over the Jordan. . . . And these stones shall be for a memorial to the children of Israel forever.

JOSHUA 4:5-7

As the children of Israel came out of the wilderness, the Lord miraculously opened a way for them to cross the river Jordan to possess the land He had promised. He instructed them to make a monument so that the children in generations to come would ask what the stones meant. The point is emphasized that the succeeding generation(s) would need to hear the story of how the Lord had brought His people, notwithstanding all their struggles, into His place of promise and purpose for their lives. The stones were not only to commemorate their history but also to assimilate a grasp of God's nature. He is the God who opens a way and brings you *through* to receive His promises.

At Christmastime one year, I made a gift of a mortar and pestle to each of our children. I put with it the simple written story of the reason for giving this gift and the hope that it might become an ornament in each of their homes. Our children knew the story, but I wanted our grandkids to be reminded of how God had changed the direction of my life—from pursuing my goal to become a pharmacist (which I knew was other than His purpose for me) to answering His call to enter pastoral ministry. That memorial I gave my children, just like the stones in the Jordan, has a story to tell about how the history of our family was shaped and how we were brought into the fulfillment of His intent for us as a family. The mortar and pestle are reminders that *life works* when you let God open the way before you and guide you so that He can bring you into a place of promised possession, power and purpose.

Tell your children the story of how God led you and brought you into a new—and better—place in your life. Perhaps it has something to do with your home or where you live. That's what the children of Israel were told to memorialize—how God led them to a home. Share with your children the story of how the Lord guided you when you weren't sure which way to go, but you believed that He had a promise for you and would fulfill it if you trusted and followed Him.

5. Tell Your Children About How God Has Delivered You

Therefore, because of . . . what had happened to them, the Jews established and imposed it upon themselves and their descendants

and all who would join them, that without fail they should cele-
brate these two days every year . . . throughout every generation,
every family, every province, and every city . . . that the memory
of them should not perish among their descendants.

ESTHER 9:26-28

In the ninth chapter of Esther, we come near to the con-
clusion of that marvelous account of how the nation of
Israel would have been demolished in a single ancient
holocaust were it not for God's intervention. A whole
nation was spared, so they established a feast they called
Purim, which is celebrated by Jews around the world to
this day. It was a great deliverance in that nation's history.
The central theme of Purim is that *our family would not even
exist except for this mercy of God.*

When I was born, by reason of peculiarities related to
my birth, I had a muscular deformity. The doctor administered regular therapy to me, but his prognosis, initially
unspoken, was that eventually this condition would take
my life. My parents weren't Christians at that time, but a
relative knew of a church where people prayed for healing
and sent a note telling them about my condition. Not
knowing that prayers had been offered to the Lord on my
behalf, on their next visit to the doctor with their afflict-
ed child, the doctor was astounded when he examined me.

He told my parents, "Mr. and Mrs. Hayford, this baby is well. I don't know what has occurred, but this is not the result of anything that has been done by my treatment." The doctor was Jewish and was unhesitant to suggest the mercy of God was at work. He further explained what he had not told my parents before—that he had no doubt that the deformity would progress in its distortion of my physical frame and would one day take my life. "What you have received," the doctor said, "is a gift from God of the life of this child."

One morning when I was about three years old, I woke up and although I don't remember the details of the episode, somehow I fell down. I tried to walk and fell down again. There was a national epidemic in the mid-1930s of poliomyelitis. This was long before the gracious intervention of medical gifts of God (such as vaccines) delivered through human instruments. There was little question of what was happening. My folks carried me to their doctor—a different one, since we had moved. After his examination confirmed their fears, he told them to take me to the hospital, saying he would meet them there.

By this time in my life, my folks were Christians (interestingly, they had received Jesus at the same church that had prayed for my healing when they did not know the Lord). As they were preparing to leave the doctor's office, they said politely to the doctor that they would like to stop by the church before going to the hospital because they wanted to have the elders pray for me. The doctor became livid—absolutely infuriated. He told my parents they could go to the hospital whenever they were ready and that he might be there or he might not, because he was too busy for this kind of nonsense.

Mamma and Daddy did stop by the church, and the pastor, along with one of the elders, came out to the car. There was a meeting going on at the church and, wisely, my folks and the pastor decided not to take me in because of the possibility of contagion. Still, without fear, the pastor and the elder laid hands on me and prayed for me with my parents. Let me pause to emphasize something: My parents had not told the doctor that they were refusing to bring me to the hospital; they just wanted to stop by the church first. Theirs was not the so-called faith that rejects medical aid or acts in a presumptuous manner. But they did make the Lord their point of first resort. It is a story of faith applied.

After praying for me, Pastor Teaford, a very wise man known for his biblical exposition and faithfulness to God's Word, gave my parents special counsel. He told my folks to take me home, put me in bed and call the doctor later. He said, "If you try to let this little boy walk now, he will be afraid, since he has fallen down every time he has tried to do so today. Take him home and let him lie down for a nap. When he wakes up, he will forget his fear. He will be able to walk again then." That's exactly what my folks did and it is exactly what happened. When I woke up, I got up and walked. All signs of polio were gone. What had been confirmed by the doctor's medical diagnosis had been allayed by the miracle intervention of God.

I have told our children and grandchildren these stories. Today, successive generations—our kids and grandkids—have their testimonies as well, and as a family we have been led to remember God's life-sparing, healing power. Let's all celebrate those things as part of our family heritage! Everyone has accounts to tell of lives being spared—mercies of God that have brought us safely thus far. Tell those stories—and bless your children.

6. Tell Your Children About God's Judgment and God's Mercy

Hear this, you elders, and give ear, all you inhabitants of the land! Has anything like this happened in your days, or even in the days of your fathers? Tell your children about it, let your children tell their children, and their children another generation. What the chewing locust left, the swarming locust has eaten; what

the swarming locust left, the crawling locust has eaten; and what
the crawling locust left, the consuming locust has eaten.

JOEL 1:2-4

Here's what the prophet was saying: *Explain to your children*
the judgment that is coming on the land because of sin. Joel was
speaking in the context of an agricultural society whose
crops were being chewed up and destroyed by insects
because of the sins of the people. Joel instructed the people
of God to explain what was happening to their children.

We must take responsibility for teaching our children
that human sin, like the insects in the fields, *chews* at our
world and leads toward the destruction of a society.
Interpret for your children, in language they can understand, what is going on in the world around them and
why it is happening.

But there is more to do with this.

First, as Joel did, call your children to pray for the
nation; show them how to pray for a dying world. By cultivating in children a compassionate heart for the lost, we
will avoid raising a breed of religious prudes who sneer at
a world and its perversion, its abortions and its other sin-
ning. We need to raise children who understand the evil
in these things, who choose to be holy—totally sold-out
for the purposes of God—but who also learn to weep in

prayer over their own generation. Teach your kids to pray for the lost.

Second, in the spirit of Joel's prophecy, which pointed toward a glorious expectation when God is sought in such a declining culture, teach your children how the Lord will pour out His Holy Spirit and they—our sons and daughters—will prophesy. Let's teach our kids to expect God, in His mercy, to pour out the power of the Holy Spirit upon them, to make them spokespersons for Him in a world being broken by the disintegrating works of sin and Satan.

Loved ones, there is a need for us to hear the counsel of the Word of God and to teach our children about these things:

- God's salvation to us
- His provision for us
- His great grace to us when we rebel or fail
- His commitment to bring us into the promises He has for us
- His sparing of lives and healing of bodies—of giving our family its existence
- Our call, especially within these devastating times, to be a praying, Holy Spirit-filled family who are agents of change in a world that needs people just like them

The Ultimate Blessing

The ultimate blessing of our children isn't only what they inherit from us, but it is also what they pass along to their kids—enriched by the addition of their own testimonies of God's grace. The key to establishing this continuing transmission from generation to generation is to do what the Scriptures command: Tell God's wonderful works—in your family, in your generation. Unlike the will that our attorney prepared, in which Anna's and my material assets would be divided into smaller portions and ultimately diminished, the groundwork may be laid for our children's spiritual inheritance to multiply with each generation. By hearing and learning of God's ways and works, being touched by love and taught by practical truth with grace and wisdom, the inheritance will thrive! And it lives on and on in the hearts of the kids we have blessed and who become a blessing in their generation.

May God make each of us—as adults influencing kids and/or as parents with our own children—people who bless our children. As believers in Jesus Christ, may our primary goal in spiritual parenting transcend the world's preoccupation with material and educational needs. Our children are worthy to be served by parents who care. But foremost, let us carve a pathway in their thinking and living that helps them become vessels of honor, who live their lives with Kingdom purpose and meaning. May we so achieve this by God's grace that they also become fountainheads of Holy Spirit blessing to others, true beneficiaries of God's glorious will and, like all Abraham's offspring, a blessing to the nations.

That's the inevitable, joyful fruit of blessing our children.

Prayer

Heavenly Father, I desire to bless my children as You so richly bless me—with love, provision, guidance, forgiveness, wisdom, hope and a sense of wholeness about who they are in You. I desire for my children to walk in Your ways, to love and serve You and to know the intimate fellowship of Your Holy Spirit. Teach me to declare to them Your wondrous works in my own life; open my eyes to see Your hand in every nuance of my day and to impart that blessing to them, so they may bless the generation to come. Lord, I thank You for the children in my life; I commit to being a faithful steward of their lives and a spiritual parent who wills to them that inheritance which is incorruptible, undefiled and does not fade away—reserved in heaven just for them. In Jesus' name I pray. Amen.

Note

1. Edwin McConnell, "Whosoever Meaneth Me" (1910).

Empower Your Life with Prayer

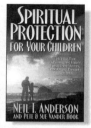

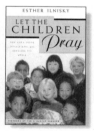

More from Jack Hayford

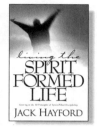

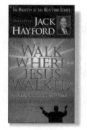
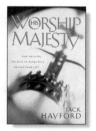